P9-CFP-496

Guderian

John Keegan

BB

Editor-in-Chief: Barrie Pitt
Editor: David Mason
Art Director: Sarah Kingham
Picture Editor: Robert Hunt
Consultant Art Editor: Denis Piper
Designer: David Allen
Illustration: David Penney
Photographic Research: Carina Dvorak
Cartographer: Arthur Banks

Photographs for this book have been especially selected from
the following archives: Bundesarchiv, Koblenz, Sado Opera
Mundi, Brussels, Ullstein, Berlin, Radio Times Hulton Picture
Library, London, Imperial War Museum, London, US National
Archives, Washington, Novosti Press Agency, London, Public
Archives of Canada, Ottowa, Heinz Guderian Collection, Bonn,
Keystone, London, Rijksinstituut, Amsterdam, Tallandier,
Paris, Suddeutscher Verlag, Munich, Zeitgeschichtliches
Bildarchiv, Munich

SBN 345-03385-X-100

First Printing: July 1973

Printed in United States of America

Ballantine Books Inc.
201 East 50th Street
New York, N.Y. 10022

Contents

Vain Endeavor

Introduction by Barrie Pitt

A study of the career of General Heinz Guderian offers an oddly chilling picture of the profession of arms. Few men reached the topmost pinnacles of their professions for the obvious reason that the pinnacles themselves are few, but the way to the top in the military life is beset by more – and more fatal – dangers than any other. The aspiring general must not only be professionally adept, he must also frequently – especially when young – place all his efforts and aspirations in hazard in order to demonstrate possession of that prime essential for a military career, physical courage. To have become a general, therefore, one must have been lucky as well as diligent.

Certainly Guderian could count himself lucky that he had come through the appalling trials and stresses of the First World War (he joined his regiment as a Second Lieutenant in 1908) with neither his health nor his intellectual powers impaired; certainly he considered himself lucky to be chosen as one of the 4,000 officers in the diminutive 100,000 man army allowed to Germany by the Treaty of Versailles.

But almost immediately he was to challenge his good fortune in a manner which in any other army or com-

bination of circumstances could well have terminated his career; he exhibited signs of wishing to become technical innovator. In England at about the same time Captain Liddell Hart was forced out of the Army and Colonel J F C Fuller was having an extremely rough passage, while in France (according to his own account Major Charles de Gaulle was laying the foundations of a lifetime's personal unpopularity – all in the same manner and in pursuit of the same vision, the restoration of mobility to a battlefield dominated by gunfire.

The German commanders in the First World War had been unusually slow in appreciating the potentiality of the Tank, and it was not until the closing months of the war that a few badly designed German tanks came lumbering onto the battlefield, then to break down or quickly to fall easy prey to the omnipresent artillery. was not surprising that Guderian attempts to translate the 'Inspectorate of Transport Troops' to which he was posted in 1922 into an embryo Panzer Corps should meet with opposition, or that even as late as 193 his retiring chief should chide him with the remark 'You're too impetuous. Believe me, neither of us will see German tanks in operation in our

6

ifetime.'

The rise of Hitler, of course, changed all that – and although with the benefit of hindsight it may be possible to see that any promotion or advancement cause by that appalling phenomenon was bound to be fatal, it was not so obvious at the time. Guderian's star waxed and by 1938 he was a Lieutenant-General at the early age of fifty, the acknowledged expert in the most favoured, most rapidly expanding and potentially most decisive arm of his service. It seemed that all his efforts would now be seen to have been justified and that supreme opportunities for the practice of his chosen speciality would be placed before him.

Certainly command and responsibility were to be his, but not always when he wanted them and always under the dictator's curb. On the coast of France after perhaps the most spectacular (and certainly the most unexpected) advance in modern warfare, he was forced to stand idly by and watch the British Army escape from as well-planned and executed a trap as military history has to show, and at the gates of Moscow he was ordered to turn away and wear the remaining guts out of his hardworked panzers in the sweep down to Kiev which to the end of his life he regarded as unnecessary.

Nevertheless, his performance when opportunity allowed amply supports the contention that he was one of the great armoured commanders of the Second World War; that his professional competence was of the highest order; that the large majority of his military theories were proved correct; that his physical courage to the end of his life was exemplary, and that his loyalty to his country, to his profession and to his comrades-in-arms of whatever rank was such that he would argue with the demonic and infuriated Hitler even while enemy armies surrounded Berlin and every man's life depended on the dictator's whim.

And what did all this dedication, diligence, imagination, competence, integrity and loyalty bring him? It brought him the spectacle of the country he loved twice humiliated, the army to which he devoted his life twice defeated, the bitter reflection that all his thought and effort, and all the blood and bravery of those who had followed and supported him, had failed to bring the only justification of the military life – victory.

Perhaps his only real good fortune was one shared by all of us – the inability to see even a week into the future.

Origins of Blitzkrieg

Blitzkrieg – lightning war – was a German conception. But when was the idea conceived? Certainly well before it was put into practice against a bewildered Polish army in September 1939, for the easy co-operation between all arms of the service and the wealth and quantity of equipment which the German army displayed in that opening campaign spoke of years of preparation. Was the new theory of war the result of Nazi influence upon the German staff mind, of Hitler bringing to the Bendlerstrasse some of the dynamism with which he had charged German economic life during the first years of his dictatorship? Or was it perhaps the stimulus of new technology, whose potential German industrialists had always shown themselves so ready to grasp, to which the generals responded? Or had the bitter juices of defeat, swallowed for a decade of foreign occupation, dissolved the traditional hostility to change and renewal in the German army? Clearly some powerful chemistry was at work, to transform the old horsey, high-collared, hierarchical *Kaiserheer* into the bustling, mechanical (indeed machine-mad) and matey Wehrmacht

Germany's desperate effort for victory: the March offensive, 1918. A section of the line at Villers Bretonneux

of which Goebbels' war correspondents wrote so enthusiastically to the German people.

Challenge, a new vision and the desire for revenge had each undoubtedly played a part in impelling the post-war German army to adopt the strategic and tactical system which, in its developed form, came to be known as Blitzkrieg. But there is evidence to show that the essentials of the system had been established, and indeed been tested in action, before the end of the First World War, yielding brilliant short-term – if ultimately disastrous – results. On the same grounds it may be argued further that blitzkrieg, far from being an adaptation of tactical principles to the special qualities of the tank, was originally a tactical substitute for that very device, an improvisation seized upon by an army which had dismissed the tank at first sight as an unpromising gadget, a mechanical toy too vulnerable to find a permanent place on the modern battlefield and which, too late, had come to realise its mistake. That it had realised its mistake it publicly confessed by trundling out on to the battlefield, at the very end of the war, a few examples of its own first and badly thought-out efforts at tank design.

The tank, as the world knows, was a British invention, though not one as exclusively British as British military historians often suggest, for the French were close behind with their own models when 'Mother' first appeared, and both it and they owed their inspiration to an American machine, the Holt caterpillar tractor. But it was certainly the British who designed the vehicle best adapted to the conditions of trench warfare: 'Mother's' specifications particularly stipulated a trench crossing capacity. It was the British who brought the tank quickest to ˮthe production stage, and they therefore were the first who were able to commit it to action.

Its earliest foray on to the battlefield, on the Flers-Courcelette sector of the Somme front on 15th September 1916, during the penultimate stage of the battle of the Somme, yielded results which were neither decisive nor even particularly spectacular. Of the forty-nine machines made available for the attack (virtually all there in existence), only thirty-six appeared at the start line, and of these less than a dozen successfully accompanied the infantry to their objectives. The rest broke down, ditched or were knocked out by shell fire. Break-downs and ditchings were common accidents to these early tanks. Their big, primitive engines ran hot at the best of times and easily overheated, while their great length which was necessary to give them a trench crossing capacity, also meant that they were very difficult to extricate if they did get stuck.

Those Germans who did meet tanks face to face on 15th September were badly frightened by them; a former subaltern of the 12th East Surreys who followed Tank D17 down the village street of Flers told the author in 196 that he took the surrender of some soldiers of the 4th Bavarian Division who were blue about the face and trembling with terror. But it was only a minority of Germans who saw a tank in that battle, either operational or disabled. None was of senior rank and since the attack of 15th September left the configuration of the Somme front largely unchanged, higher German headquarters formed the opinion that the tank could be discounted as a weapon of war. Its significance was compared to other novelty weapons that trench fighting had produced such as flamethrowers; unpleasant and unsettling accompaniments to infantry attacks, but purely local in effect, and not, as the British tank pioneers were beginning to perceive of strategic, perhaps even war-winning significance. This German judgement was reinforced by their experience of later tank attacks, mounted in greater strength, during the spring, summer

A British Mark 1, one of the first to appear on the Somme battlefield

nd early autumn of 1917. 'The German roops', their official historian wrote, soon learned to know its vulnerable arts and attack it accordingly. The ow speed, small numbers and large arget surface of the tank of this eriod made it a comparatively easy rey for the artillery which, after a hort time, detailed special guns to ngage it.'

If this passage suggests compla-ency it is probably no accident, for he German army had indeed become omplacent by the end of 1917, about oth its power to hold its front against lllied attack in the west and its bility to clean up meanwhile the ubsidiary fronts in the east and outh-east of Europe. All the greater, herefore, the shock to its self-esteem nd sense of security inflicted by the ritish break-in at Cambrai on 20th ovember 1917. There, in a single norning, a six-mile section of the

Hindenburg Line was bitten out by a quite small force of infantry, five divisions, attacking without artillery preparation but behind a screen of 300 tanks. An unforeseen delay in the timetable of the advance, the fault of a British divisional commander hos-tile to the new weapon, prevented the British from transforming this break-in into a genuine break-out through the German rear areas, while their prevailing lack of infantry reserves caused them to lose the short battle of attrition which followed. They had nevertheless demonstrated, in a fashion to which the German High Command could not shut its eyes, that the secret of breaching the Western Front had at last been found.

But the Germans, almost at the same moment, had themselves been

11

A line of British tanks advances towards the Cambrai Front and the first conspicuously successful tank tank attack in history

putting the finishing touches to a front-breaking system of their own. At Riga on the Baltic in September and at Caporetto on the Italian front in late October they had proved to themselves that they had hit upon workable solution. They were now preparing to demonstrate it against the French and British, and at the earliest possible moment, for the imminent arrival of the American army threatened to reverse the balance of numbers against them for good. As it was, they would enjoy numerical advantage, brought about by the collapse of the Russian army which had made possible the transfer of their eastern army – less all but a token occupation force of older men – to the west for the first six or seven months of 1918.

It was vital, therefore, that the new tactics should work. And no intellectual effort had been spared to see that they did. For, unlike the Allies, the Germans were not looking to a mechanical innovation to break the deadlock for them; as we have seen, they had largely ignored the possibilities which automotive technology offered. Instead, they were depending on a refinement of established artillery techniques and a new system of infantry deployment. Combined, these methods took the form of what western armies would come to call 'infiltration tactics'. The resulting programme of attack was to go, ideally, something like this.

The preliminary bombardment, which by British or French practice ought to have lasted several days, was to be drastically curtailed. And for an obvious reason: it had always betrayed the exact location and, within narrow limits, the timing of a

Captured Russian machine-guns and mortars in Riga

Russian soldiers who deserted from the front in 1917

Grisly relic of the Italian defeat at Caporetto

oming offensive. Rightly recognising that surprise is the prerequisite of a successful break-in, the Germans had developed a technique of 'silent registration' which eliminated the need for newly-emplaced batteries to test-fire their guns to see that they were on target, and yet permitted the large concentrations of artillery, which it was necessary to build up in the attack area, to draw up fire plans which it was certain would work 'on the day'. Hence was made possible the secret assembly of what the Allied High Command would come to call 'Luden-dorff's battering train'.

This battering train was provisioned for a shattering bombardment and barrage. For although the duration of the bombardment was to be short its weight was to be very intense indeed, intense enough in its effect upon human nerves and human physique to compensate for the very much lesser material damage that it would inflict, compared with a normal barrage, upon the defensive structure of the enemy's front. German gunnery experts specifically distinguished between the results of the two sorts of artillery bombardment: that produced by the now traditional, very protracted fire programme, which they called 'destructive', and that to be produced by their own new method, which they called 'neutralising'. The object of the two methods, by their analysis, was quite different: whereas the destructive bombardment was supposed to crack off the protective carapace of dugouts, concrete pill-boxes, wire and supporting artillery positions which encased the front-line soldier, leaving him exposed to a fatal thrust by the assulting infantry who would follow the barrage, the 'neutralising' bombardment was designed to attack the nerves and senses of the front-line soldier *through* his hard shell of fixed defences, assailing his eyes, lungs and skin with gas and his nervous system with an unheralded and unprecedented volume of noise, blast and vibration. This neutralising bombardment was to fall on battery-positions and cross-roads, as well as front-line and support-line trenches, with the object of disabling, either physically or mentally, each and every component of the enemy's defensive system. As soon as this result had been achieved – it was thought that from four to six hours shelling would be sufficient – the first waves of infantry would leave these positions and move forward.

Their attack formation would bear no resemblance, however, to those which the Germans had learned to mow down with such regularity during the Allied offensives of 1915–17. No long lines of evenly-spaced, slowly-moving infantry would present themselves as targets to those British or French soldiers who still retained the power to handle their weapons. All they would see instead would be glimpses of small groups of lightly-clad Germans darting from one place of cover to another across no-man's land and then, having secured entry, disappearing rearward. These small groups, the

spearhead of the offensive mass which would follow, would be drawn from the *Stoss* ('stab' or 'thrust') troops of the attacking divisions; these were specially trained and equipped soldiers having something of the function and prestige which commandos and rangers were to achieve in the Second World War. Since the end of 1917 each German division had been ordered to select a company of picked soldiers young, fit, experienced and with a record of aggressiveness. They were to be equipped with a specially lightened machine-gun (the 08/15, with sub-machine guns where available (usually the Bergmann), with the Mauser carbine instead of the rifle and with pistols and fighting knives. Tactically they were organised into what we now call a section, comprising a gun-group and a rifle-group: the gun group *(Maschinegewehrtrupp)* consisted of a two-man machine-gun team and two ammunition carriers, the

General Ludendorff and his wife

**German shock troops
advance at the double through
a breached barricade**

rifle-group *(Stosstrupp)* of seven rifle-men. Acting together in mutual support, the gun group would cover the advance of the riflemen to a point from which they, in turn, could assist the gun-group to move up. If seriously impeded, the two groups could call on the assistance of flame-thrower and light-mortar teams which followed close behind. Behind them again other teams would be dragging forward light artillery pieces. And to their rear, moving in great solid grey wedges would march the masses of the follow-up divisions.

Not only was this a particularly well thought-out tactical system.

**German machine-gun nest prepare s
to give supporting fire for the storm
troops' attack**

German assault detachment moves in with a flame-thrower

What made it even more menacing to the Allies was that the *Stoss* troops, on whose determination the success of the whole would largely depend, had already acquired a ferocious self-image and an extremely high standing within their own armies. They would, in short, need neither to be driven nor even led forward, but would depart forwards under their own impulsion. An observer has described this new breed of soldier (new, because the spirit of the pre-war German army was inimical to the display of initiative by enlisted men): 'he did not march with shouldered rifle but with un-slung carbine. His knees and elbows are protected by leather patches. He no longer wears a cartridge belt but sticks his cartridges in his pockets.'

Below: Mortar teams follow closely behind the storm troops' advance

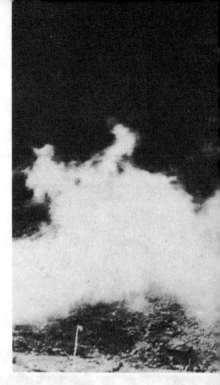

Crossed over his shoulders are two sacks for his hand-grenades . . . Thus he moves from shell-hole to shell-hole, through searing fire, shot and attack, creeping, crawling like a robber, hugging the ground like an animal, never daunted, never surprised . . . always shifting, cunning, always full of confidence in himself and in his ability to handle any situation.' One of their officers, analysing the *Stoss* troops' motivation, later wrote: 'The turmoil of our feelings was called forth by rage, alcohol and the thirst for blood. As we advanced heavily but irresistibly towards the enemy lines, I was boiling over with a fury which gripped me . . . the overpowering desire to kill gave me wings. Rage squeezed bitter tears from my eyes . . . Only the spell of primaeval instinct remained.'

In the military long-term, the creation of the *Stoss* troops was to prove a mistake, by concentrating the mos aggressive soldiers of a formation in group which was likely to suffer th heaviest casualties, the fighting valu of the whole would eventually bu inevitably diminish. In the politica long-term, too, the creation of th *Stoss* troops was to yield the graves consequences. Many of the survivor became, in a remarkable phrase c Hermann Göring's, 'fighters wh could not become debrutalised', an though the bands of right-wing volur teers *(Freikorps)* later recruited fror the *Stoss* troops were to be instrumenta in the suppression of the communis rebellions in Germany after th revolution of 1918, they were also t form the nucleus of the Stormtrooper who kept German politics in a stat of endemic turmoil throughout th nineteen-twenties and helped to carr Hitler to power in 1933.

In the military short-term, howeve

he *Stoss* troops were, within the larger actical formula which Ludendorff's taff had devised, to win for Germany series of successes so large in scale hat it seemed by mid-1918 that she as on the very brink of victory. eginning in March of that year, her rmies had unleashed one offensive fter another on the Allied line, each f which had brought all but total ollapse to the troops which stood in s way.

The first, that of 21st March, was imed at the junction of the British nd French armies, just south of the omme, and struck directly on the ritish Fifth Army. This, the weakest f Haig's armies, was occupying ositions only recently taken over om the French and which were ultily designed and badly construc- d. Its staff, moreover, had mis- nderstood the scheme of defence to hich the French had been working –

one which expected the position to be held 'in depth' and which they and the British, as it happened, had copied from the Germans – and had put far too many of their soldiers into the forward positions. This was all that the Germans could have hoped for – tactically the equivalent of the 'kindly favour' which Schlieffen prayed the French would do him – as they did by attacking his left wing – in 1914. Thus it was that when the *Stoss* troops appeared out of the mists on the morning of 21st March (the mist was a stroke of luck and a very important one) they found the British trenches either undefended – their occupants being so demoralised by the opening bombardment that they could not man their fire-positions – or else held only by badly shaken and already isolated parties of men who could usually be induced to cease resistance when they learned that their flanks had been turned.

Pressing onwards into the British positions, the *Stoss* troops and the vast crowds of conventional infantry following them in the second wave now began a fighting advance. This was to culminate in the effective destruction of the Fifth Army (its number was removed from the order of battle during the re-organisation which followed the offensive), the only just averted separation of the British from the French armies and the greatest command crisis (itself the reflection of a severe shaking of morale at the highest level) which the war had produced on the Allied side, or was to again. For on 26th March Field-Marshal Haig, perceiving no other way to ensure the participation of the French reinforcements from Pétain's as yet untouched reserves of which he was in desperate need, agreed – indeed proposed – that he be subordinated to an inter-Allied Commander-in-Chief. The man chosen to occupy this new post was the French General Foch. In

Field-Marshal Sir Douglas Haig

General Foch

agreeing to this subordination, Haig was voluntarily taking a step which he had fought against since assuming command of the BEF in 1915, one which he had always equated with the surrender of British military autonomy and much national – to say nothing of personal – prestige and which only the fear of a much more humiliating surrender in the open field could have induced him to contemplate.

At the moment that the Allies were reaching this unwilling agreement the Germans were approaching Amiens after an advance of twenty-five miles in five days – a pace and depth of penetration unknown in France since the open warfare of August and September 1914. Almost immediately afterwards, however, the impetus of their advance began to diminish. They had themselves suffered enormous casualties – approaching a quarter of a million out of an attacking force of eighty-eight divisions – and of course most of these losses had been borne by

the infantry. Calculating the avera[ge] infantry strength of a German nin[e] battalion division at 6,300, it seer[ns] that death or wounds must ha[ve] struck down nearly half the soldie[rs] engaged. And an examination of t[he] casualty returns of individual di[v]isions bears out that hypothesis. T[he] 1st Battalion, 140th Regiment, of t[he] 4th Division had, by the end of t[he] offensive, only three officers and 1[..] men left with the colours; a battali[on] of the 64th Reserve Regiment, of t[he] 1st Guards Reserve Division, lost [all] but eighty of its men between 21st a[nd] 24th March; and the 40th Fusiliers [of] the 28th Division lost two-thirds [of] its effectives between 21st and 28[th] March. All three were first-rate form[a]tions and would have suffered m[ore] heavily than most. But the patte[rn] was common to good and bad divisio[ns] alike. And among its more disturbi[ng] features was a very heavy casual[ty] rate among officers, heavier than an[y]thing the German officer corps h[ad] suffered since 1914 and all the har[der] o make good because entry to the corps, the social apex and political bastion of the Imperial system, had been artificially restricted even during the war. (NCOs promoted to officer functions were not allowed officer titles but were called *Offizier-stellvertreter* or *Feldwebel-leutnant*.) These losses could not be made good, and without trained, energetic young leaders the success of future offensives would be very unsure.

But the March offensive had lost its momentum for other reasons besides casualties, vital though that factor was. Among those other reasons was the unforeseen difficulty of the terrain which had been chosen for its execution. For behind the British front of 1918 lay the 'Old Somme Battlefield', a devastated area over fifty miles square, criss-crossed with abandoned trenches (the homes throughout 1917 of tough gangs of deserters which the military police never succeeded in rinkling out) and rusting barbed wire entanglements, often concealed by thickets of dank grass, and pitted by millions of shell holes. The British, quite lacking the labour to clear up this wilderness (it had fallen entirely into their possession following the German withdrawal to the Hindenburg line in March 1917) had done no more than repair the more important roads which crossed it, together with their bridges and culverts. These, easily demolished by the sappers of the British Fifth Army during its own retreat, could not be repaired at speed by the advancing Germans, and their columns of transport and artillery had had to spill over therefore into the devastated zone and try to pick across country. The infantry had found it difficult enough to make headway; the drivers of the horsedrawn guns and waggons found it almost impossible. The consequences were to be disastrous. For while British dumps could be looted for food and drink (an expedient which caused more difficulties than it solved when those dumps contained ration rum), the

military as opposed to the human needs of the army could be supplied only from its own rear areas. Without those supplies, particularly of shells for the few guns which had been able to keep up with the leading infantry, the German assault had no edge. Thus it was that scratch British garrisons, which would have been swept away in the first two or three days of the offensive, proved strong enough a week later to delay and eventually to halt it. German staff officers, tracing the outline of 'ground gained' on their situation maps at headquarters, watched helpless as it assumed the shape of a gradually narrowing pocket. Allied staff officers, whose maps during the first days had made no sense at all, were able a week later to draw with some confidence a firm new line around what they knew to be their own positions and which, though running in an ugly bulge, no longer threatened to disintegrate and burst its contents all over the British zone.

Four factors had contributed to this stabilisation (and stabilisation meant defeat, of course, for the German offensive): losses among elite troops; losses among junior leaders; inability to ferry forward essential supplies across open country; inability readily to deliver large-calibre at the point of assault during fluid operations. In a military analysis, the failure of the offensive lay not in the conception (though the choice of a front of attack which, if all went well, would extend to include the Old Somme Battlefield does not speak highly of German planning skills) nor in the execution of the attack, but in the exploitation of its initial success.

Inability to sustain the momentum of an attack beset all armies in the First World War, but so horrific were the other tactical features of most operations that this one in particular escaped the attention of all but the most perceptive professional observer. Others found it unnecessary to look beyond the initial rebuff almost always inflicted upon the leading

waves ('They're hanging on the old barbed wire') to find an explanation for failure, or to the lack of destructive effect of the artillery preparation, or to a delay in bringing reserves to the most decisive sector. And indeed it is in these familair terms that one can explain the failure of the four German offensives which followed the great March battle. That of April, against the British in Flanders, broke down in familiar style, though it gave Haig some bad moments before it did; the May offensive, against the French Chemin des Dames front, made a good deal of ground but eventually failed for want of reinforcements of which the Germans were now running short; the June offensive on the Matz was in any case a deliberately limited affair; and the July offensive, unwisely given the public code-name 'Peace Offensive', was smartly counter-attacked by a

eft: A casualty is carried from the battlefield. *Above:* The offensive in full wing, June 1918. *Below:* Horse-drawn artillery in difficult terrain on the Old Somme Battlefield'

fresh and well-briefed French army and thrown back in confusion. Nevertheless, a trained eye would still have picked out that pattern of features, later to be brilliantly encapsulated by Liddell Hart in the phrase 'the diminishing power of the offensive', and argued that it was these, rather than any of the more obvious setbacks, which lay at the root of the German failure.

The Allies were about to demonstrate, moreover, a new tactical system which would avoid the paralysing grip of that 'diminishing power'. The German retreat after the Second Battle of the Marne in July had carried them back to the line of the 'old western front' on almost the whole length of the French sector. It now remained for the Allies to reduce the vast Somme salient, won from them by the Germans in March. Towards the end of July they began to assemble opposite it a great army, which included for the first time in the war a mighty force of French as well as British tanks. The British tanks, it is true, were still very much more numerous than the French, 534 to 72, and all the French tanks were of the light Renault type. Light tanks, of which the British had 120 ('Whippets') were, however, as necessary an ingredient of the Allied plan as heavy, for the hope was – as always in the First World War, but on this occasion with some real expectation of success – to advance quick and deep through any breach which the first shock of the assault might make.

Reality transcended expectations. The Germans, confronted with column after column of tanks emerging from the morning mist of 8th August, simply abandoned their trenches and fled to the rear. Their commanders, accepting the impossibility of reversing the situation, ordered the artillery to limber up and follow. The great columns of retreating troops thus formed provided the Allied airforces with magnificent targets at th crossing-places over the river Somm at the back of the battlefield. An such reinforcements as the Germa could find to march up and hold temporary line were greeted by th sheep-like cries of those running awa – the first warning detected by th German high command that th morale of their men had begun crack on a large scale.

By 10th August the impetus ha run out of the Allied attack, in pa because they too had now run u against the obstacle of the Old Somm Battlefield, but mainly because of th very large number of tank brea downs they had suffered. On th evening of 8th August, only 145 of th original 414 fighting tanks were st 'goers', and on the following day third of these also fell out of action one way or another. The air force too, had suffered heavy losses. In t first two days of the battle they ha

French Schneider tanks entrain

French Chaumond tanks

enjoyed air superiority, and had profited from it to intervene in the land battle on a scale and with an effect never before seen on the Western Front. Amiens, indeed, if not the first great tank battle – that title belongs to Cambrai, as we have seen – was certainly the first great land-air battle, with the air forces seeking at last to perform that role which the artillery had tried – and failed – to do for so long: to 'interdict' the battlefield, i.e. to prevent the approach of fresh troops towards the critical focus of the fighting. In this, the airmen had been only partly successful, though given the means at their disposal – the small, low-endurance and lightly armed aircraft of the period – their achievement had been admirable. But by the third day, when large reinforcements of German squadrons, including the Richthofen squadron under the command of Hermann Göring, had arrived in the vicinity, the air battle reverted to the more traditional type: a struggle for command of the sky in the tactical zone. In it, neither side secured a clear advantage.

A further factor in the deceleration of the Anglo-French advance was the failure of signal communications. Of course, signal communications had always failed in the battles of this war for, dependent as they were upon a system of telephone cables, buried towards the rear but necessarily carried over the surface in the front line and forward of it, almost any of the millions of violent acts which occur in a battle, from the explosion of a shell to the heavy tread of an infantryman's nailed boot, could interrupt a vital link in the network. Not merely could but did: hence the additional burden of signal flares and pigeon-baskets which so many infantrymen carried across no man's land, these unsatisfactory expedients providing the only alternative means of communication between front and

Canadian armoured
cars go into action
during the battle of Amiens

rear, between infantry and artillery, between lieutenants and generals, once the wires were cut.

What drew the attention of the staffs to this familiar breakdown was that even the emergency expedients failed to work on this occasion, the distances over which they had to operate being so very much greater than any known in a comparable period – that being a function of the speed and depth of the Allied advance. Moreover, to emphasise how unsatisfactory was the existing state of affairs, the first transportable wireless sets had just made their appearance. Bulky and unreliable, they nevertheless demonstrated, when they could be coaxed to work, that tactical communication in

battle was capable of a complete transformation.

The shortcomings in their own offensive methods perceived by the British and the French would have been of little comfort to the German high command. Although they had lost little ground – about twelve miles in depth, inconsiderable in the context of 1918 – they had felt the fighting spirit of their army wilt and had witnessed the emergence of a new kind of offensive effort which they lacked the means to counter. For the Germans, though they had (very late in

Hermann Göring in his tri-plane cockpit in 1916

the day) embarked on a tank-building programme of their own, had no hope of equipping their armies with tanks in the numbers possessed by the Allies, nor did they possess an effective anti-tank weapon. Little wonder therefore that Ludendorff was to call 8th August 'the black day of the German army' or that the German official historian would later call Amiens 'the greatest defeat which the German army had suffered since the beginning of the war'.

Thereafter the German army suffered nothing but defeat. Its withdrawal from one line of resistance to another across the plains of northern France was orderly; but the plain fact was that it was going in the wrong direction, which the high command knew it could not reverse. The sueing for an armistice and the cease-fire to which it led in November were therefore the logical and inevitable outcomes of the disasters of the late summer. And the armies which filed back across the

Rhine bridges in the month following 11th November 1918 were in truth defeated armies, whatever legends patriotic Germans would later comfort themselves with.

But one group at least within the German army remained undefeated: the survivors of the pre-war officer corps. Now that they had lost their Kaiser, to whom they had pledged their loyalty, they had only a single focus for their corporate devotion left to them: the army itself. Some would interpret the demands of that devotion in terms of the need to preserve the social exclusiveness of the officer corps; others in the need to re-establish liaison with the forces of popular patriotism within the German nation; others again, perhaps the majority, in the need to preserve the army's supra-political role. A few, of whom a young staff officer named Heinz Guderian was one, were already looking to re-establish the German army's technical and professional superiority over all others in Europe – the cachet which it had enjoyed in 1914. In the divers elements to which the war had

Above: German troops lay field telephone wires to connect advance infantry units with headquarters. Below: Captured British tanks in use by the Germans before they embarked on a tank-building programme of their own

given birth, or which it had invested with military significance – the tank, the ground-attack aeroplane, the radio set, 'infiltration' tactics – officers like Guderian perceived the making of a new way of warfare. They were determined to make that way German property.

Their ultimate achievement was to be even more dazzling than they could have foreseen in the grey days of defeat and revolution at the end of 1918. Not only were they to weave out of those elements the new way of warfare which they glimpsed. They – or those who twenty years later were to watch them put it into practice – were to give it a German name which has entered into the vocabulary of the world: Blitzkrieg.

Above left: French and British soldiers and civilians celebrate the news of the Armistice. *Below left:* The last German troops cross back into German soil over the Rhine. *Below:* The Kaiser with his wife in exile

The lessons of defeat

Heinz Guderian was born, the son of a German regular infantry officer, on 17th June 1888. He came of traditional German officer-class stock, his paternal and maternal grandfathers being both landowners from eastern Germany, and he was given the traditional education of a German officer's son. At the age of twelve, when his father was stationed at St Avold in occupied Alsace-Lorraine, he was sent off, with his ten-year-old brother, to the cadet school at Karlsruhe in the kingdom of Baden. There he stayed for two years and in April 1903 was transferred to the Main Cadet School (Haupt-Kadetten-Anstalt) at Gross-Lichterfelde, near Berlin. Guderian describes his training as characterised by 'military austerity and simplicity . . . but founded on kindness and justice'. We must understand these words in a very relative sense. The upbringing of all children in western countries was a good deal more severe before the First World War than it is today. But even by contemporary standards, the regime in the German cadet schools was Spartan. Unlike America and Britain, which then as now selected their potential officers at the age of eighteen or so and sought to equip

Sports day at Guderian's military college

Heinz Guderian as a schoolboy with
his mother and younger brother Fritz

oung Guderian during training at the
adet school in Karlsruhe

them with a college education, the German empire plucked its future second-lieutenants almost out of the nursery and confined them for six or seven years of their childhood and youth within a strict and exclusively military environment. Their teachers were serving officers, their nurses hard-bitten NCOs of the Imperial Army; and, perhaps most oppressive of all, the overseers of the minutiae of their everyday lives were their own seniors, invested with authority as cadet officers. It was a system which had a counterpart perhaps only in the scheme of training of British naval officers; and it illuminates the peculiar importance of each service to its own country's world position, strategic requirements and ultimate national survival that this stern, anachronistic schooling was defended so vigorously by those who had passed through it and accepted so fatalistically by their wives when the time came to surrender

their fledglings to its cold embrace.

It was an embrace which could crush a sensitive spirit. But Guderian was tough material, besides being intellectually outstanding. He passed successfully through all stages of his cadet training, did his statutory attachment to the 10th Hanover Jäger Battalion, which his father was then commanding, and, having undergone the convention of election to the regiment by its officers, was commissioned into it as second-lieutenant on 27th January 1908.

In view of Guderian's subsequent career, his choice of regiment, influenced though it was by family circumstances, was not without significance. For the Jäger – Light Infantry or Rifle – Battalions of the Imperial Army were expected to perform in war the role either of reconnaissance troops to an infantry corps, being equipped with a plentiful issue of bicycles for the purpose, or of support

the battle honours of the King's German Legion, the Hanoverian cotingent of the British Army which had fought Napoleon in the Peninsula and at Waterloo. It had in fact no historical right to do so, the Hanoverian army, which was the true descendant of the King's German Legion, having been disbanded when the Kingdom of Hanover was annexed by Prussia in 1866. But it was a pretence which pleased the Kaiser and it produced the odd result that in 1914 German and British regiments bearing identical battle honours from the Peninsular War found themselves face to face in the firing line.

Guderian was not however to witness that clash. When the 9th Cavalry Division marched westward in early August 1914, with the 10th Jägers under command, he was commanding a wireless station in the headquarters of the 5th Cavalry Division in the Third Army. Command of a wireless station was an unusual and responsible position and he would not have achieved it if he had not already made his mark as an officer of promise. This he achieved by winning selection to the *Kriegsakademie* – the German Army Staff College – in the competition of 1913. Training at the staff college was an essential ingredient of the career of any officer who hoped to rise. There was intense rivalry for places and Guderian had done well to be selected so young. At the outbreak of war in 1914, the current course at the *Kriegsakademie* was dissolved and the students distributed to suitable staff appointments. As Guderian had a period of attachment to a signal battalion before joining the academy, the wireless station post was an obvious one for him to have been given.

German army personnel policy dictated that staff-trained officers should alternate regularly in their appointments between 'staff' and 'command', and one would therefore expect that

roops to a cavalry division. In either ase, their role was to be a mobile one nd, like the Rifle regiments of the ritish army or the French *chasseurs*, hey affected to regard the 'heavy' nfantry as slower than themselves in nind as well as body. Whatever the ubstance of that conceit, the Jäger attalions, though not standing parcularly high in the complicated ocial hierarchy of German regiments, ere extremely good troops, and their nen, who were selected as far as possle from foresters and mountaineers, ere trained to show an independence f action in the field which was not xpected from conscripts of the line egiments.

Guderian's battalion was stationed t Bitche, in Lorraine, when he was rst commissioned into it. But in 009, it returned to its home province f Hanover, to join the other regiments f the X Corps. This formation, by nperial decree, had since 1891 adopted

**Lieutenant Guderian with his wife
Margarete and son Heinz, August 1915**

Guderian, after completing his attachment to the 5th Cavalry Division's wireless station in April 1915, should have returned to his regiment, perhaps as a company commander. Instead, he was transferred as Assistant Signals Officer to the headquarters of the German Fourth Army with which he remained, with intermissions, until April 1917. He had meanwhile been promoted Captain and was then chosen to leave signals work and take up a General Staff appointment with the 4th Infantry Division, then holding a sector opposite the French sector of the front in Champagne. And from thence until the end fo the war, with the exception of a single month spent as commander of the second battalion, 14th Infantry Regiment, he was to serve solely in General Staff appointments. He rose continually, being promoted from the staff of a division, to a corps, to an army, and eventually, in February

1918, to the General Staff of the Army, a distinction which admitted him t the charmed circle of German militar life and conferred on him the privileg of wearing the outward sign of hi election, the carmine stripe on th seam of his trousers. At the end of th war he was serving in the most pres tigious of all German staff posts, tha of Ia – General Staff Officer, Opera tions.

That appointment in October 191 had taken him to Italy, his first mov away from the Western Front sinc the beginning of the war. He did no therefore witness the withdrawa from France and Belgium which fo lowed. He was however to be instantl and totally involved in the problem which armistice, withdrawal and de mobilisation brought in their wak Of these by far the greatest in mag nitude was the evaporation of th German Army. Its commanders ha formed the view, as a result of it exemplarary maintenance of disc pline during the withdrawal from th occupied territories in the West, tha

Guderian as captain with German
Fourth Army, 3rd Division, 1917

it had, following the temporary disorders of the last weeks of the war,
returned to its ancestral loyalties.
Once home, it demonstrated that its
reputation for obedience had been
merely a convenient device, calculated to ensure its return in the
swiftest possible time. It did so by
'voting with its feet'; individually or
in small groups, the soldiers of the
German army simply left their bar-
racks, almost as soon as they reached
them, and went back to their families.
By the end of December 1918, the new
German republic had almost no regular
soldiers left under its command at all.

This posed very serious problems.
Revolution was abroad in Germany,
not simply the sort of anti-war dem-
onstrations which had prodded the
General Staff into dismissing the
Kaiser, but organised movements
aiming at genuine social upheaval.
Berlin was threatened with civil war
and Munich, the capital of Bavaria,
was in the hands of a socialist government which, pink rather than red
though it was, looked Bolshevik

scarlet to the Prussian middle classes.
Political reaction, whether from the
left or the right, was a certain out-
come; and if it was not to lead to the
breakdown of order and the fragmen-
tation of the German state, the new
Republic would quickly have to provide itself with a loyal and efficient
armed force.

This was certainly the view taken
by the new Greman Government, and
even more strongly by the General
Staff, which for a week or so found
itself in the absurd and invidious
position of lacking an army over
which to exercise command. This is
not to say that every last unit of the
old Imperial army had disappeared. On
the contrary, nearly half a million of
its soldiers were still under arms.
But their stations of duty lay far to
the east, in the territories annexed
from Russia at the imposed peace of
Brest-Litovsk. And between the annexed Ukraine, where the majority

Above: German armour is demolished following demobilisation. *Below:* Berlin is threatened with civil war after the German defeat, 1918

stood, and the frontiers of Germany stretched a great belt of territory under the control of no properly constituted sovereign authority. Some of this territory was the property of the former Austrian Empire, which had collapsed two months before. Some was German territory over which Berlin lacked the means to exercise authority. And the rest was formerly Russian, from which the Tsarist or Bolshevik administration had been driven by German military action between 1914 and 1917.

Had it been a simple power vacuum in the region with which Berlin had to deal, the recall of the eastern army would have been a simple affair to arrange. But the situation was by no means a simple one. Eastern Europe was up for grabs and at least nine parties – the Russians, Poles, Czechs, Germans, Estonians, Lithuanians, Latvians, French and British – were involved in the scrimmage. This list takes no account of the disorders in the Balkans, where the South Slavs were disputing their boundaries with their former Hungarian overlords, or of the civil war in Russia, or of the Ukrainian separatist movement, or of the only recently settled Russo-Finnish conflict – the parties to each of which had a direct interest in the nature of any settlement of frontiers for Poland and the Baltic states.

The Poles had most to say on the matter, and the loudest voice, which was amplified at the conference table by the French, who saw in the reconstitution of a large, powerful Poland the chance to acquire a permanent and strategically placed ally against Germany. Diplomatically, Germany had no case to muster against Polish and French ambitions; unlike both, however, she had forces on the ground. And in the former Russian coastal provinces of Lithuania, Latvia and Estonia, racially non-Russian and historically heavily penetrated by

Russian field kitchen in Poland, 1920

The Würtenberg Freikorps

German influence, she could find bases from which to exert military counter-pressure against Polish expansion northwards towards the sea and – more important – westward towards Prussia and German Silesia.

As things turned out, the force which Berlin had counted to draw upon for defence both of her interests in the east and of the republican government at home began to exhibit in early 1919 all the symptoms of dissolution which had overcome the *Westheer* in December. Out of the ruin of the old Imperial army, however, something new was arising to take its place: the *Freikorps*. These bands of hardened 'front-fighters' had disparate origins; some were regiments of the old army which for some reason or other had kept their cohesion; some were brought together by common nationalist or counter-revolutionary feeling; some followed a charismatic leader; some were simple mercenaries; no doubt there was a good deal of overlapping of motive in most.

One of the most effective units was that raised in Latvia from the remnants of the German army there. Christened the Iron Brigade by its leader, Major Bischoff, it covered the retreat of the fugitive Germans to Riga and later, when the General Staff began to implement its decision to make a major military effort in the east, became the principal instrument of its strategy in the Baltic states. While various *Freikorps* operated in Silesia and Prussia to restrain the infant Polish army from engulfing too much of historic German territory, the Iron Brigade – soon expanded enough to justify its renaming as the Iron Division – began an offensive into Lithuania and Latvia. By May, when Guderian had been posted to the staff of the Iron Division, the Germans were poised to occupy Riga, principal port and city of Latvia, having driven out a Bolshevik incursion. The Allies

had now become alarmed, however, for although the provisions of the November armistice enjoined the Germans to keep the peace in the east (by which 'defeat the Bolsheviks' could be understood), the nascent Latvian government had succeeded in persuading the representatives at Paris that Germany had embarked on a campaign of conquest, aimed at least at establishing puppet governments in those states where, by the Wilson rules, 'national self-determination' should decide the future.

Diplomatic and naval action ensued. And though not swift enough to avert the re-occupation of Riga, it did bring about both the cessation of German military operations and the reinforcement of the tiny native Latvian army. When the Iron Division, resuming the offensive under the pretext that it was not a force under the control of the central German government, met the Latvians in battle in late June, it was defeated. Following on that, the German commander in Latvia was

orced to agree to the withdrawal of ll German troops from the Baltic egion. Germany's last minute attempt to compensate herself in the east or the humiliation she had suffered in he west was thus set at nought. She vould have to reconcile herself to an astern Europe in which three Baltic tates flourished independently, a najor Polish state ruled over much istoric German soil (and a good many terman nationals) and, hardest of all o bear, East Prussia was separated rom the rest of Germany to provide 'oland with access to the sea at Danzig.

Guderian returned from Latvia to ake up a staff appointment in Hanver, his home military district. 'ending the announcement by the .llies of their firm proposals for the isarming of Germany, the Weimar overnment had formed a 'Provisional *eichswehr*', a skeleton model of the

Major Bischoff, leader of the Iron Brigade

German troops on the Baltic before the unsuccessful battle with the Latvian army. Note the early use of the swastika

old Imperial army. Thus the old twenty-four Corps districts were preserved, but its contingent was now reduced to brigade strength. The X Army Corps was therefore replaced by *Reichswehr* Brigade 10 – though like many of the new brigades it had at first considerable difficulty in filling out its numbers. Several of the brigades were in fact formed by designating *Freikorps* as official government troops. Once Berlin had re-established control however and had been able to demonstrate that its legitimacy was recognised by the general staff, recruiting became brisker. Indeed, competition to join the *Reichswehr* soon became intense; there was indeed little alternative employment for many ex-servicemen. This was particularly true of the ex-Imperial officer corps, whose members

had temperamental and ideologica objections to finding employment ou side the 'profession of honour'.

It may be understood, therefor with what horror and outrage th officer corps heard the detailed mil tary provisions of the Versaille Treaty. For these proposed a pe: manent reduction of the strength the German army from the figure about half a million (to which it ha climbed, if one includes the *Freikorp* by June 1919) to that of 100,000; on 4,000 of whom were to be officers. Th cadet schools were to be closed (thu destroying, the Allies intended, th nurseries of the Prussian office caste), the *Kriegsakademie*, its un versity, likewise, and the Grea General Staff, its directing brai: dissolved. On the material sid Germany was to be denied heav artillery, tanks, aeroplanes and a but the barest stocks of warlike store

Since rejection of these terms woul have invited a French and Britis invasion, which Germany could n

have hoped to resist successfully the army and, almost as reluctantly, the government reconciled themselves to accepting them. Now began for the army the agonising process of deciding which of the many thousands of applicants should be chosen for the very few permanent commissions which would be open in the 'hundred thousand' army. Even though Germany had been very sparing in the granting of war-time commissions, and despite the very heavy losses among officers, about 32,000 had returned from the front fit for duty. This meant that only one in eight of those available could be chosen. The overt criteria adopted were those of evidence of courage in combat and of suitability for promotion to 'the next higher step in case of war'; covertly, the army was also keen to pick candidates with an aristocratic background. Guderian, whose combat experience was limited and whose family circumstances were middling rather than upper class, was not an obviously hopeful contender.

Officers watch the signing of the Versailles Peace Treaty which sought a permanent reduction of the strength of the German army

But his reputation as a staff officer turned the trick. At the end of 1919 he was confirmed as an officer of the new Reichswehr.

After two years regimental duty with his old battalion, he was assigned in January 1922 to the recreated General Staff (camouflaged for treaty purposes as the *Truppenamt*), a posting which surprised him, he modestly admitted, since vacancies in it were so rare. The branch to which he was posted was one quite unfamiliar to him: the Inspectorate of Transport Troops. On and off, he was to remain with it for thirteen years, during which time it was to evolve into the parent branch of the Panzer Corps. The posting was thus a fateful one, not only for Guderian personally, but also for the German army, for without his vision and persistence the development of the Transport Troops might not have taken the turn he helped to give it.

First detached, in order to gain some practical experience, to a transport battalion in Munich commanded by a Major Lutz, with whom he was to establish an important friendship, Guderian spent the years 1922–4 in Berlin, accumulating a fundamental working knowledge not merely of the characteristics and limitations of motorised units but, by extension, of the theory of tank operations as well. He was guided in that direction by his conclusion that, since Germany's weakness would force upon her a strategy of mobile defence in the event of war, tanks would have to be employed in order to cover the motorised transport columns which would feed the fighting line. Eager for all the information he could find on the subject, he soon came across the pioneering writing of the two English tank theorists, J F C Fuller and Basil Liddell Hart, who were themselves striving to transform British thinking about future warfare. From the latter in particular, he acknowledged learning of the possibility of long-range armoured strokes, aimed at the enemy's communications, and delivered by formations containing both tanks and motorised infantry. 'Since nobody else busied himself with this material,' he wrote, he began to publish some articles of his own in the German military weekly, and as a result 'was soon by way of being an expert'.

The attention he attracted in this way, and also by his organisation of an exercise in ground-air operations, led to his being nominated in October 1924 as an instructor in tactics and military history on the staff of 2nd Division. This post, and its counterparts in the other divisions, were elements in a training system which had been designed to substitute for that provided by the abolished *Kriegs-akademie*. Being forbidden to bring together its most promising officers

for General Staff training, the *Reichs-wehr* achieved the same effect by dispersing the best available instructors among the formations. Guderian in gravitating to his 2nd Division appointment, was therefore receiving a professional accolade of the highest sort.

Guderian was free to choose his own instructional examples, and naturally concentrated on subjects which reflected his own interests, including the French and German cavalry operations in 1914 – the last great exercise in mobile warfare. His continuing concern with mobile operations was noted by his superiors, and on the conclusion of his instructional appointment in October 1927 he was returned to the Transport section of the General Staff at Berlin where a job had been specially created for him. He was to study the problems of troop transportation by truck. But he was soon asked to continue his instructional work, this time with fellow members of the Transport Department, and to take as his subject matter the operational use of tanks.

From now on, Guderian was to occupy himself more and more consciously – and openly – with the creation of a German tank force Having experimented at Berlin with tank dummies – canvas, and later sheet metal contrivances manned by soldiers of the 9th Regiment – and having done an attachment to a Swedish tank battalion, he was posted in February 1930 to command a Motor Transport Battalion, his first regimental appointment for eight years But both he and Lutz, his friend of 1922 and now his superior in the Transport Branch, had rather more ambitious plans for the battalion than 'carrying flour' – all that an earlier superior had thought transport units fit for. One of his four companies was at once equipped with dummy tanks, one as an anti-tank company one with motor-cycles and the fourth with armoured reconnaissance cars At first Guderian had little luck in

tting this armoured reconnaissance
ttalion of his – for this in effect was
hat he and Lutz had made it – em-
oyed in a meaningful role. But in the
ring of 1931 the then Inspector of
ransport Troops, General Otto von
ülpnagel, after uttering the all-too-
vallowable words, 'You're too im-
tuous. Believe me, neither of us will
er see German tanks in operation in
ur lifetime', retired, to be succeeded
r Lutz – now promoted general.
Authority was now on Guderian's
de, for Lutz took his side entirely in
e struggle for 'new tactical develop-
ents'. But Lutz had larger plans for
m than command of an experimental
ttalion. In October 1931 he called
uderian to Berlin to be his chief of
aff. The two now embarked on a
volutionary programme. It had two
rposes, interdependent and of equal
nportance. One was to provide the
erman army with a panzer (ar-
oured) force. The other was to
rsuade the traditional fighting arms
' the German army, the infantry and
e cavalry, of the operationally
cisive role that tanks could play.
Guderian and Lutz, their guns un-
asked, now began to encounter
xactly the same weight of opposition
at the tank pioneers in England, and
• a lesser extent in France and
merica, already knew well. Resist-
ce to this form of innovation sprang
. part from a genuine failure of belief
. the decisive capability of armour,
it also from instincts of institutional
lf-preservation. The British cavalry
ared that the expansion of the Tank
orps would entail the extinction of
eir own historic regiments – a fear
hich the more ferocious tank en-
usiasts gleefully fed. In Germany,
pposition was perhaps less parochial
an in England, but Guderian com-
ains that it was real enough. The
spector of Cavalry told Lutz in 1931
at he was still thinking of using his
rce as a shock arm on the battle-
eld, and was prepared to allot only
reconnaissance role to armoured
its. His successor, General Knochen-

The English tank theorist, Colonel
J F C Fuller

hauer, was less generous. He had
formed Germany's three Versailles
cavalry divisions into a corps and
intended to capture the armoured
reconnaissance battalions for it. Lutz
and Guderian were able to stave him
off. But they had to fight on other
fronts too. The cardinal doctrine of
the 100,000 army was that of 'yielding
defence' – all, indeed, of which an
army of that size would have been
capable against her contemporary
enemies. 'This method of fighting a
battle,' Guderian comments with
unusual bluntness, 'is invariably
marked by extreme confusion, and I
have never seen an example of it that
was marked by anything but extreme
confusion.' Unfortunately its chief
advocate within the army, General
Beck, became commander-in-chief
shortly after Hitler's accession to
power; and rightly seeing in Lutz's
and Guderian's plans a scheme of
warfare which ran directly counter to
'yielding defence', he attempted to
stifle them by restricting the future

RW-3135

le of armour to infantry support by units of at largest brigade strength. Guderián and Lutz, however, found at they had in the new Nazi Chanllor an ally who could disregard the cooperative Beck. Hitler had no built grasp of the importance of nks, but as soon as he had seen one Guderian's units in action, in the urse of a demonstration at the Army 'dnance Establishment at Kummersrf, he recognised that he had found e weapon of the future. 'That's what eed! That's what I want', he repeatly exclaimed, Guderian tells us, as watched the Panzer I tanks, moured cars and motor cycles show ' their speed and precision of movent.

Hitler was, of course, about to ibark on his programme of open -armament. (The programme may may not have been part of a secret

moured cars built of flimsy sheet etal presage the beginning of the rman Tank Force

General Lutz, centre, and Guderian eventually succeed in persuading the German Army of the operationally decisive role of armour on the battlefield

deal with the *Reichswehr* in return for which it lent him its tacit support, but in any case it was enormously popular both with the services and the nation.) The seven divisions of the 100,000 army were to be expanded to twenty-seven. The *Kriegsakademie* was to be re-opened. Conscription – at first only for a term of twelve, later of twenty-four months – was to be introduced. And, what from Guderian's point of view was crucial for Germany's military future, the decision was taken to include in this programme of expansion the formation of three panzer divisions. By 15th October 1935 they had come into existence, and command of the 2nd, at Würzburg, was given to Guderian, still only a colonel.

These first panzer divisions were very improvised organisations, with

General Knochenhauer

makeshift equipment – which would have been a great deal more makeshift had the *Reichswehr* (now the *Wehrmacht*) not eluded the restrictions of the Versailles treaty on the design and development of tanks by setting up an experimental station in Russia, with the complicity of the Red Army. As a result, although the panzer divisions were issued at first only with the Panzer I – an almost unarmed training vehicle – and the Panzer II – a light tank with a 37mm high-velocity gun – the much more formidable Panzers III and IV were already projected and under development. And in terms of organisation and numbers, the early panzer divisions were on a lavish establishment, with four tank battalions each, three motorised infantry battalions, a reconnaissance battalion, an artillery regiment an, anti-tank battalion, an engineer company and a signal battalion. This very plentiful provision for signal communication within the division reflects

both Guderian's early training as signal officer and his recognition the advantage which quick and flexib means of contact between hea quarters and subordinate units co ferred on the commander. Division generals in the First World War ha frequently, indeed normally, issue orders on the basis of intelligence least four or five hours old, if no older, and since their orders coul then take as long again to reach th front, they were often unfulfillable irrelevant. Guderian intended to er sure that in an armoured battle th delay in transmissions should k reduced from hours to minutes. Indee he saw no other way of managin modern mobile operations except b radio control from wheeled hea quarters located as close to the from as possible. This style of comman later to be known as 'forward control would eventually be adopted by ever modern army. Guderian had not ye glimpsed its most developed form. Bu he knew that the old, slow deliberativ method was outdated, and Beck complaint, 'But you can't comman an army without maps and telephone Haven't you ever read Schlieffen? only confirmed him in his view.

By 1937 Guderian's whole theory the future of tank operations w sufficiently far advanced for him feel ready to put it before the arn and the public. It was outlined in short book with the arresting title *Achtung! Panzer* (*Attention! Tanks*), t meat of which he outlined in article in the German officer's pr fessional journal of that Octobe What is fascinating about the artic is the direct line of descent whic Guderian traces between the almo successful German tactics of infiltr tion of 1918 and the *blitzkrieg* he for saw. 'The March offensive of 1918 w outstandingly successful,' he wrot 'despite the fact that no new weapo were employed. If, in addition to th normal methods of achieving surpris new weapons are also employed, the the effects of surprise will be great

Armoured car and tracked armour during manoeuvres. Motorised armour earns recognition as the weapon of the future

Guderian as commander of the 2nd Panzer Division in Würzburg

increased.' But he went on to deny that the justification for introducing new weapons – the large panzer formation in this case – was merely that it would enhance the effects of surprise. On the contrary, he argued, the contribution tanks could make was much larger, and one that no other arm could offer. 'We believe that by attacking with tanks we can achieve a higher rate of movement than has been hitherto obtainable, and – what is perhaps even more important – that we can keep moving once a breakthrough has been made.' This last crucial point was where, as we have seen, the German offensives failed in 1918. It would be vital, however, to keep the tanks concentrated in large formations: 'an infantry division with, say, fifty anti-tank weapons can stand up far more easily to an attack by fifty tanks than to an attack by 200. We conclude that the suggestion that our tanks be divided among infantry divisions is nothing but a return to the original English tactics of 1916–17, which were even then a failure, for the English tanks were not a success until they were used in mass at Cambrai.' But, 'if the attack is carried out with sufficient concentration, width and depth we shall destroy recognisable targets as they present themselves' – a sideswipe at those artillery officers who were planning week-long preparatory bombardments – 'and thus drive a hole in the enemy's defences through which our reserves can follow more speedily than was possible in 1918. We want these reserves to be available in the form of Panzer Divisions, since we no longer believe that other formations have the fighting ability the speed and the maneouvrability necessary for the full exploitation of the attack and breakthrough.'

A message implicit in Guderian's argument was that Germany's three existing Panzer divisions were too few and that the three so-called Light Divisions formed concurrently – a sop to the cavalry clique in the army – should be converted to a true tank role. But Guderian, though now a major-general – he had been promoted in 1936 – was not yet influential enough to bring that about. In 1938 however, the progress of his career was to accelerate dramatically, largely as a result of the Blomberg-Fritsch crisis. Those two officers, respectively Minister of War and Commander-in-Chief were both revealed in early February to be compromised in their personal lives. The revelations in Blomberg's case were correct – he had made an unsuitable second marriage – but in Fritsch's case were a fabrication, the product of a decision by Hitler, or those about him, to profit from the opportunity that Blomberg's indiscretion offered to break the independence of the high command, the only organisation still outside Nazi control and still in a position to challenge it and replace the dishonoured officer.

General Beck

56

General Fritsch, left, and General Blomberg, dismissed by the Führer in 1938

by others more pliable. Guderian's old patron, Lutz, was a minor victim of the resulting purge, and Guderian was nominated to succeed him – reading the news, he tells us, in the newspaper. He was immediately promoted lieutenant-general and in November, following the bloodless occupations of Austria and the Czech Sudetenland, full general. He was just fifty. In the *Reichswehr* the average age of colonels had been fifty-two.

In between his rapid promotions he had held the appointment of Commander of the XVI Corps, that controlling the three panzer divisions. His promotion to general (*General der Panzertruppen*, in the German style) carried with it a new appointment,

that of Commander of Mobile Troop a supervisory post overseeing t development of panzer divisions, t bastard 'light' divisions and t remnants of the cavalry. It was a j for which Guderian had little tas since in its creation he suspected attempt by the high command, still his view inimical to the 'panzer ide to neutralise its principal prota onist, himself, by involving him routine administration. He demand and obtained an interview with Hitl at which he explained why he thoug it so necessary for him to reta undivided authority for the devel ment of the panzer force and asked be returned to his old post. Hitl

Hitler speaks at the Hofburg in Vienna following the bloodless occupation of Austria

refused him – but invited him to report personally if he felt he was being hindered from fully discharging his new responsibilities which, Hitler emphasised, were for the development of the whole mobile arm. Guderian accordingly fell in with his wishes.

From an objective point of view, it was the right decision. Guderian, like many enthusiasts, tended to see prejudice where none existed. And although there were undoubtedly senior officers in the army who did not share his faith in the potential of the panzer arm, it was a rapidly expanding branch of the service. By January 1939 he had five panzer divisions in existence, with the prospect of forming a sixth; the light divisions, now four in number, were capable of rapid transformation to full armoured status if necessary; the Mark III and IV tanks were coming out of the factories; and the seizure of the rump of Czechoslovakia would shortly deliver much excellent Czech equipment into his hands. If it came to war, Germany's armoured strength would put her on close to an equal footing with any of her neighbours, except Russia. But then Hitler was not thinking of attacking Russia – yet.

59

The welcome given to German troops in the Sudetenland

Lightning victories

Exactly when Hitler came to a firm decision to attack Poland remains a matter of debate. Like all German nationalists, he detested the Polish state which Versailles had created, both because of the formerly German territory which had gone into its making and because of its major role in the French plan to encircle Germany with watchdogs. He was also committed by the ideology of his party to the winning of *lebensraum* in the east – and *lebensraum* most easily translated itself in German ears to mean the historic areas of colonisation on the now Polish rivers Memel and Vistula. On the other hand, it would be very difficult to show that the extinction of Poland was a long-term Nazi objective; if, that is, one is looking for hard black and white evidence. Rather is it more meaningful to say that by 1939 the most pressing of Hitler's problems, in his judgement, was the 'solution' of Germany's unsatisfactory eastern frontier; and that the determination of Britain and France, strengthened by their cowardice over Czechoslovakia the previous summer, to withhold their assent from a second carve-up only reinforced his will to have his own way.

He could not have it, however, without making concessions somewhere. And since by March Britain had publicly committed herself to guaranteeing the integrity of Polish territory (which effectually committed France), he could now only win the freedom of

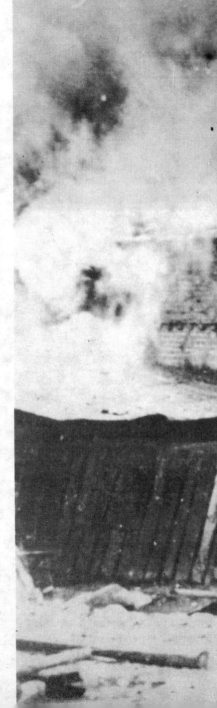

Polish defeat by the German invader seems a certainty

lations with the Soviets. In both cases there had been an element of Hobson's choice involved, since an understanding with Russia was the only one available both after 1870 and 1918. But special circumstances apart, a Russian treaty always made sense for Germany, and never more so than in 1939, when she had incurred the hostility of Britain and France and was committed to a course of action which would eventually prompt them to bargain for Russian help if Germand did not anticipate them. Indeed, they had been so bargaining but, through the same lack of resolve which had lost them the game at Munich the year before, they had failed to clinch the deal in time Hitler was thus, quite justifiably, able to represent his new alliance to the generals as a full-blown diplomatic triumph. What that triumph implied for the Wehrmacht some of them already knew. Those who did not were let into the secret that afternoon at Obersalzberg.

The military plan, on which Runddstedt, Blumentritt and Manstein, a formidable trio, had been working since May, presupposed that, in the event of Poland's diplomatic isolation (which had now come about, British and French help being unavailing), Poland would not hold the western half of the country in any strength, but would seek to stand on the Vistula and then fall back progressively on the river lines to the east. In those circumstances, the Wehrmacht would divide its ground forces between East Prussia and Slovakia and make a concentric attack, in unison with a massive air assault on Poland's poorly defended aerodromes. It was the obvious plan and the right-plan. The existence of East Prussia, a military enclave within the territory of the Polish republic, had always given Germany, in any strategic context in which she enjoyed superiority of

ction he needed by agreement with he other great European power, oviet Russia. On 22nd August, he as able to inform his generals that e had, in return for an agreement to artition Poland between the two ountries, been successful in concluding a non-aggression pact with Russia, which gave him almost complete freeom of action in northern Europe.

This news, which might have been xpected to awaken the anti-Bolshevik nxieties of the German high command, was however by no means adly received. Two important strands German strategic and foreign olicy had always been fear of Russia nd fear of encirclement. Bismark had ade friendship with Russia a cardinal rinciple of his foreign policy during he early years of the Second Reich nd Seeckt, who had remade the erman army after Versailles, had illingly entered into military re-

bbentrop signs the Nazi-Soviet act in 1939

General von Seeckt, responsible for the rebirth of the German army after the Treaty of Versailles

numbers, an important initial advantage, for from it she could outflank Poland from the north. The recent acquisition of Slovakia, from which Germany could also outflank from the south Poland's western frontier defences, put Poland in an almost indefensible posture. Given that the French and British did not try and fight a Tannenberg – and nothing in their words or actions suggested that they would – the defeat of Poland in short order seemed a certainty.

Not that the disparity in numbers between the two armies was all that great. Allowing for the force of second-class divisions left to hold the West Wall against the possibility of France making good her guarantees, Germany could deploy about fifty-two divisions in the east, some one and a half million men in all. In round numbers, the Poles were only slightly inferior,

and could almost match the German in numbers of divisions put into th field: thirty-nine infantry divisions and seventeen miscellaneous brigades But most of these brigades were cav alry; only two were motorised; an there were no armoured divisions. I short, Poland, though possessing som tanks, had nothing to match the te: Panzer and Light Divisions whic. Germany could put into the field. No could her airforce redress the balance Although it possessed about 1,00 planes, to the Luftwaffe's 1,500 ,the; were not matched in quality, and the operated from aerodromes which wer located too far forward and too clos together and which were not ad equately defended.

It was nevertheless just possibl that by reckless action Poland migh disrupt the smooth unrolling of th German war plan. And that woul happen if her forces could prevent rapid junction between the bulk c Bock's Army Group North, located i Pomerania, and German Third Arm:

bove: German anti-tank gun in action in Poland. *Below:* Poland could not hope to
match the light divisions Germany put in the field

n East Prussia. That army would then ecome a hostage, upon whose relief he Wehrmacht would have to bend ll its efforts, meanwhile abandoning ts search for a quick decision on the ther fronts.

That, at any rate, in 'worst case' erms, was how the German planners stimated the situation. And they ad therefore made the achievement f a junction actoss the neck of the 'olish Corridor the very first priority. t would clearly have to be won by aotorised and armoured troops, and whole corps, XIX, had been assigned o the task. It was command of that orps which Guderian secured for imself, although not without diffi-ulty. For he discovered by accident hat the War Ministry had nominated im for command of a reserve infantry orps in the event of hostilities and he ad to fight to get the assignment hanged.

XIX Corps was an exciting command. c contained one of the original panzer ivisions (the 3rd) and the 2nd and 20th Iotorised Infantry Divisions. At-ached were the Panzer and Recon-aissance demonstration Battalions f the army – excellent units which ould later go to form one of the most lustrious of all German formations, anzer Lehr Division. The whole ssemblage was a true armoured ommand, of the sort for which uderian had been arguing and work-ig during the last dozen years. The aallenge now was to prove the claims e had been making for it.

Guderian's specific task was to cross ae River Brahe, just inside the olish Corridor, and drive to the istula where it formed the frontier of ast Prussia just north of Kulm – uderian's birthplace. Opposing olish strength was reckoned at three fantry divisions and a cavalry ·igade with some Fiat-Ansaldo ,nks.

On 1st September at 04.45 hours,

uderian in his armoured command ehicle

Guderian's corps crossed the frontier. He himself accompanied 3rd Panzer Division (in whose reconnaissance battalion one of his two sons was serving) in an armoured command vehicle equipped with radio – thus becoming 'the first corps commander ever to use armoured command ve-hicles to accompany tanks on to the battlefield'. (A claim which General Elles of the British Tank Corps, who had led his command in person at Cambrai, might have disputed.) The experience was not wholly happy. The Panzer Division's green gunners, firing against orders into the mist, succeeded in bracketing their corps commander, whose driver, while taking evasive action, landed in a ditch and put the vehicle out of action. Guderian retired on foot, 'had a word with the over-eager artillerymen' (not a difficult conversation to reconstruct, one imagines) and changed vehicles.

Re-mounted, he found that the lead-ing troops, who had been held up at Gross-Klonia, an estate which had belonged to his great-grandfather, were settling down for a rest, their com-mander apparently believing that no further progress was possible that day. Guderian, whose order that the River Brahe should be crossed before the end of the day had been forgotten, was just giving way to anger when he was approached by a young panzer lieutenant, who told him that in his view the Polish forces on the far bank were weak, and that a bridge to which they had set fire had been salved – by himself, as it happened. Guderian hastened to the spot, found the report accurate, galvanised the junior com-manders, and got the battle going again. A reconnaissance battalion crossed the river at an undefended point in rubber boats, secured a lodgement and made it safe for the tanks to use the bridge. Guderian then ordered the division to press on to its final objective on the Vistula.

Meanwhile his two motorised div-isions had also been behaving with some of the nervousness characteristic

The German Sd. Kfz 251/3 command car. Guderian's personalised command vehicle equipped with radio, thus becoming the 'first corps commander ever to use armoured command vehicles to accompany tanks on the battlefield'.
Weight: 8.37 tons; *Crew:* up to 12; *Armament:* one 7.29 mm machine gun; *Armour:* 12 mm maximum; *Engine:* one Maybach 6-cylinder inline, 100 hp; *Speed:* 31 mph; *Range:* 186 miles; *Length:* 19 feet; *Width:* 6 feet 11 inches; *Height:* 5 feet 9 inches.

of unblooded soldiers of even the best quality. One of the two divisional commanders informed Guderian that he was being compelled to withdraw by Polish cavalry. At first speechless, then acid, Guderian at once set off for the divisional area where, finding the staff still all at sea, he took command of the regiment which had been withdrawn and led it up to its objective. Thereafter, he tells us, the division's attack made rapid progress. So, after an initial hesitation, did that of the 20th Division.

By the night of 4th September the Corridor had been crossed and Guderian's first task was complete. From the final objective he could see the towers of Kulm, his birthplace in the days when this territory had be German.

Next day, Guderian was visited Hitler, who drove with him to inspe the scene of the fighting and the uni engaged. Stopping to view the smash equipment of a Polish artillery reg ment (it would have been of Fren pattern, with which Hitler was fa iliar from the First World War), t Führer asked if the Luftwaffe's di bombers had been responsible. 'Wh I [Guderian] replied, "No, our panzers he was plainly astonished.' He w also surprised, though agreeably, the low casualty figures for the cor during the first five days fighting some 150 killed and 700 wounded. Hit compared them with the casualti

Crossing a newly erected bridge
constructed by pioneers

s own regiment, the 16th Bavarian
eserve, had suffered in a single day's
ghting in the First World War – over
000. Guderian did not hesitate to
ake the obvious point that tanks
ere a saver of lives, as well as an
strument of destruction. He appar-
tly did not reveal, however, that his
ficer casualties had been dispro-
rtionately high. They included the
ns of the Under-Secretary at the
reign Office and a former Chief of
aff. But, as Guderian knew, high
ficer casualties are always a feature
the first battles of a war, green
oops needing a great deal in the way
self-sacrificing leadership.

There was now a short break in the
mpaign while the Germans re-

grouped, spent by Guderian in a
shooting holiday in the grounds of a
castle which Napoleon had made his
headquarters during the 1807 and 1812
campaigns (Guderian slept in his
bedroom). Meanwhile the high command drew up the dispositions for the
second stage of the campaign. It was to
be very much a clearing up stage, for
the fighting power of the Poles had
already been broken. The sky was
almost empty of their aeroplanes and
the best of their divisions were either
destroyed or in full retreat. The
need now was to encircle those that
were left in the field and to make a

Above: Kulm, Guderian's birthplace, before the invasion of Poland
Below: Grim-faced young Poles witness the German bombing of Warsaw

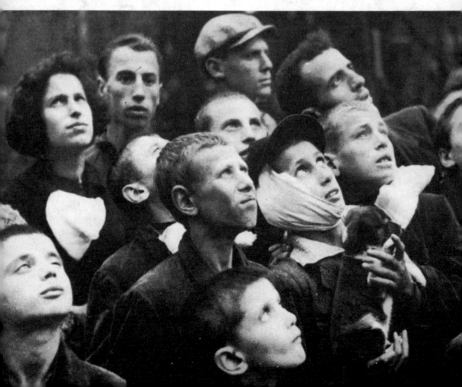

German attack on Poland, 1939

dy junction with the Russians on the river Bug (which was to be the Soviet Union's line of partition with the Germans). To that end, the Germans were to advance in four large columns, the two in the centre aimed at Warsaw but with orders to achieve an encirclement of the Polish forces to the west of the city, the two outer columns sweeping in a wide pincer movement to trap the remainder of the Polish army and join hands at Brest-Litovsk on the Bug.

Guderian was disappointed to discover that his corps was allotted to one of the centre columns, and hastened to the headquarters of his Army Group commander, Bock, to explain why he thought this an inappropriate mission. Better, he argued, to make use of the formation's long stride to direct it at Brest-Litovsk, instead of harnessing it to the slow pace of an infantry advance on Warsaw. Bock was persuaded and on 9th September Guderian led his Corps off towards the first objective, the crossing places over the River Narev. And lead it he had to in person, for once more he found one of his divisions, which should have been spearheading the advance, stalled in the very first stage of the attack. It was not through loss of nerve, but because of an over scrupulous attention to procedure – the sort of action which would have attracted favourable comment during peace-time manoeuvres but which was quite uncalled for in time of war, or at least the style of warfare which Guderian intended to teach his soldiers. Cancelling a relief of companies which he found in progress, he summoned the responsible regimental commander to him and led the officer forward until they came under Polish fire. From that point he directed the assault and then raced back to supervise the passage of the tanks of the division (it was 10th Panzer) across

the Narev. The divisional bridging company not having completed its work, the tanks had to be ferried. Guderian watched the operation begin and then left to inject some urgency into activities elsewhere. His anger may be imagined when he discovered later in the day that, by unauthorised counter-order, the bridging company had left the panzer division's sector before all the tanks were across and installed its bridges downstream for the convenience of some much more amphibious infantrymen. Since a second panzer division, the 3rd, had now arrived behind the 10th and was queueing for a crossing, the rapid unrolling of XIX Corps' attack was in jeopardy. Once again Guderian had to intervene personally. And the pattern was repeated on the following day, part of which Guderian spent so close to the Polish lines that a rumour circulated among his command that he had been cut off. The motor-cycle battalion which came to rescue him was much relieved to find him standing unscathed in the middle of the village which he had temporarily made his headquarters, on fire though it was.

Next day, by last light, reconnaissance elements of Guderian's corps reached the outskirts of Brest-Litovsk. On 14th and 15th September he disengaged the fighting elements from contact with the retreating Poles, who could now safely be left under observation by light forces, and broke through the outer defences of the city to secure its encirclement. And on 16th September he launched his attack on the citadel. It did not prove a painless experience. Brest was one of the oldest and strongest fortresses of eastern Europe and the Polish garrison fought with desperate bravery to defend it. Guderian's adjutant was shot dead from the ramparts at a range of a hundred yards and the fortifications were eventually taken only by resorting to the traditional methods of infantry fire-and-movement behind a rolling

Warsaw surrenders; a Polish envoy meets **German** officers, carrying a flag of truce

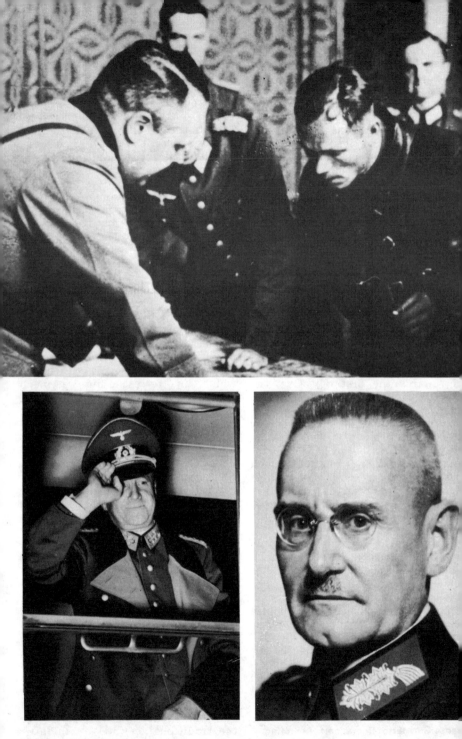

General Brauchitsch   General Halder

arrage. The events should have been warning to Guderian that there are mits to a tank's usefulness. But in he euphoria of victory – for the apture of the citadel marked the ulmination both of his own mission nd effectively of the German conquest f Poland – it may have passed him by. Guderian's forces were now inside he zone which had been allotted to he Russians by the agreement of 22nd ugust. On 17th September the first ussians appeared, to be followed by Soviet general who spoke French, which Guderian conversed with him amiably, he recorded. On 22nd eptember 'after a farewell parade and lutes to the two flags', the two enerals parted, Guderian to take part victory celebrations at Berlin. It ould not be his last encounter with he Russian army at Brest-Litovsk.

Guderian was invested, during the elebrations at Berlin, with the night's Cross of the Iron Cross (the *itterkreuz*), a decoration newly cre- ed to take the place of the former

highest Prussian award, the *Pour le Merite*. Like that order, it might be won either by senior officers for out- standingly successful conduct of op- erations, or by junior ranks for extraordinary bravery in the face of the enemy. Guderian accepted his 'as vindication of my long struggle for the creation of the new armoured force'. But the investiture ceremony was not to be his only meeting with Hitler that winter. He also had the opportunity of speaking to him at an official lunch following the ceremony and later of securing an interview with him at which he represented the dismay of the high command at the poorness of the relations prevailing between the leadership of the party and the army. Guderian, at least by his own account – which is independ- ently corroborated – was not among that very large group of officers who would not speak their minds to the Führer.

Most of the winter was spent, how- ever, preparing for the campaign against Britain, France and her neighbours. The decision for the attack was taken, or at least first revealed to an inner circle of military chiefs, in October. But it had still to be translated into an operational plan, which exercise was to occupy the high command for most of the winter. Two factors contrived to delay the opening of the campaign (three if one includes the exceptionally bad weath- er): the army staff's reluctance to put things to the test against the enemies who had beaten them in 1918; and their failure, which was in part a product of this reluctance, to produce a plan of which Hitler could approve.

The first proposal put forward by Brauchitsch, the Commander-in-Chief, and Halder, Army Chief of Staff, was known as *Fall Gelb* (Case Yellow) and was for a modified repetition of the Schlieffen Plan to which Germany had marched west in 1914. 'Modified' must

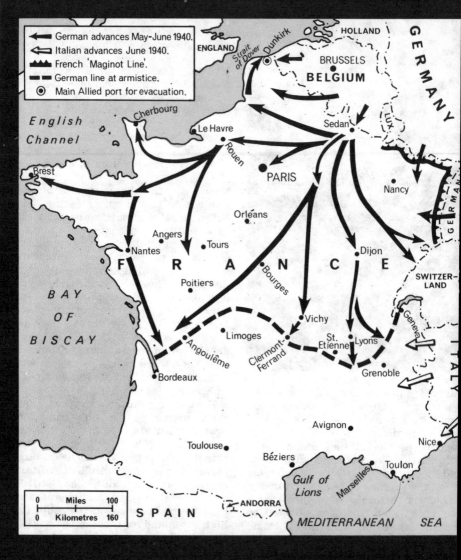

Invasion of France, 1940

be emphasised; for though the plan followed the same route as Schlieffen's – through lowland Belgium – and had the same initial objective – the gaining of the Channel coast, it lacked Schlieffen's ruthlessness of aim: the destruction of the French army at a single blow and in short order. Indeed, the paradox was that Schlieffen had proposed a *blitzkrieg* for an army which lacked the speed and mobility to achieve one; his successors, commanding an army which had already demonstrated its ability to wage *blitzkrieg*, were talking of committing it to an almost 19th century programme of campaign.

To do Halder and Brauchitsch justice, they admitted the flaws in their plan from the outset. But this self-criticism was not to compare in weight with that directed against it from elsewhere within the Wehrmacht. The most telling stroke was Manstein's. He (whom Guderian regarded as 'our finest operational brain') was still acting as Chief of Staff to Rundstedt and in that capacity proposed a radical and much more decisive scheme. The centre of attack (*Schwerpunkt*) was to be shifted from lowland Belgium to the hills and forests of the Ardennes. The bulk of the panzer divisions was to be massed there and when the assault unrolled they were to race for the crossings over the Meuse, 'mask' the end of the Maginot line (which petered out at the southern tip of the Ardennes) and then race for the sea. The additional advantage that the Germans would reap from launching their attack that much further to the south, he argued, was the much larger balance of enemy troops which they would thereby encircle. For whereas *Gelb* would scarcely have brushed the main French positions, Manstein's plan would carve straight through them, and at a point below that sector where the bulk of their mobile forces might reasonably be expected. Those mobile forces would then be constricted within an ever-narrowing pocket by the

German troops in the 'panzer corridor' and those advancing in more orthodox fashion from Belgium.

It was a good, if daring, plan, in the preparation of which Manstein had the benefit of Guderian's advice. For the former, though immensely quick and creative of mind, lacked any thorough experience of tank operations; it was a reassurance for him to have Guderian's word that the plan was workable. Manstein's next difficulty was to bring it to the attention of Hitler, which he eventually succeeded in doing only in a roundabout and slightly unprofessional way, when dining with him informally during the following February. By that time however, and as a result of a great deal of inter-staff communication, conferencing and war-gaming, Halder and Brauchitsch had themselves very much radicalised their proposals, so that their eventual scheme, submitted to and approved by Hitler in late February, was even bolder than Manstein's.

One of the formative influences upon Halder during this period was a war-game in which he took part at Army Group A's headquarters at Coblenz. There he had a noisy disagreement with Guderian about the pace at which the crossing of the Meuse could safely be forced. Guderian, needless to say, was for a breakneck breakthrough and a headlong continuation of the advance, Halder for a deliberate operation with a subsequent pause to regroup.

Events would prove who was correct, for it was precisely this mission – the crossing of the Meuse – which was to be assigned to Guderian in the final operation orders.

He remained in command of the XIX Corps, but the composition of that formation was now changed to include 1st, 2nd and 10th Panzer Divisions and the *Grossdeutschland* Regiment, a large motorised regiment of four battalions (which furnished in rotation the Führer's Escort Battalion, Rommel's command during

General von Manstein

1938 and 1939). It was an immensely powerful force, containing twelve panzer battalions – about 800 tanks, three armoured car battalions, sixteen battalions of motorised infantry and sixteen batteries of anti-tank, anti-aircraft and field artillery.

This formidable assembly of modern fighting strength was itself only part of a yet larger one – Panzer Group Kleist, which had under command, besides XIX Corps, both XLI Panzer Corps and XIV Motorised Corps: in all five panzer and three motorised divisions. This, the 'Sunday punch' of Rundstedt's Army Group A, was to be flanked to the north by another two panzer divisions, 5th and 7th, the latter commanded by Rommel. This left only three panzer divisions, 3rd, 4th and 9th, for Bock's Army Group B, which was to engage the French and British when they made their expected advance into the Low Countries, and none for Leeb's Army Group C, whose role was to be a more or less static one on the Maginot Line sector.

Guderian's initial and crucial attack objective lay just north of the end of the Maginot Line, at Sedan on the Meuse. His task was to cross the difficult country of the Belgian Ardennes as quickly as possible and seize crossings over the river. Zero hour was set for 10th May and it was not expected that, on his sector at any rate, the enemy would offer much initial resistance.

And so it turned out. While parachutists and bombs rained down in a deluge on the Dutch and Belgian defenders of the northern lowlands, instantly attracting northwards the mobile divisions of the French field army and the British Expeditionary Force, Guderian advanced almost unnoticed and barely opposed into the Ardennes forests. On the morning of 12th May Rifle Regiment 1 of 1st Panzer Division, commanded by an archetypal fire-eater, Colonel Hermann Balck, seized bridgeheads across the Semois, an eastern tributary of the Meuse, and that evening

German tanks form up for the push into the west, 1940

the commanders of 1st and 10th Panzer Divisions were able to report that they had captured the city and fortress of Sedan – a name of semi-mystical significance in modern German history, for it was the fall of that city in 1870 which marked Prussia's victory over France and confirmed her leadership of a unified modern Germany.

Capture of the city did not, however, open a way across the Meuse, for the French had naturally blown the bridges before their capitulation. Bridgeheads would therefore have to be seized the following day by assault crossing, and for this operation Guderian had made the most careful plans and preparation. Perhaps the most important were his arrangements and understanding with the Air Group attached to the Army Group. He had

General von Kleist

The swift German advance into Belgium

invited the Luftwaffe officers to all his conferences and, after much discussion, had eventually secured their agreement that the most mutually profitable task the airmen could perform would be to attack or constantly threaten with attack the French batteries covering the Meuse, later to be nullified by higher orders for a mass bombing attack, which luckily arrived too late for the plans to be changed.

The first successful crossing of the river, under this protective air umbrella, was to be achieved by Balck's Rifle Regiment. Noting that the French defenders opposite, though sheltered by thick concrete emplacements, seemed shattered by the latest air attack they had undergone he ordered up the trucks carrying his collapsible boats, assembled them under the eyes of the Frenchmen opposite, less than fifty yards away, and launched his riflemen across the stream. They landed almost unscathed and took the position. When Guderian arrived shortly afterwards, Balck greeted him with the words, 'Joy-riding in canoes on the Meuse is forbidden' – which was a remark Guderian himself had levelled reprovingly at some young officers during a training exercise which he did not think they were taking seriously enough.

The foothold secured, Guderian could now order bridging, enlarge his lodgement on the far bank and prepare to break out. His superior, Kleist, was by no means sure, however, that a continuation of the advance was the right or safe thing to do. Inevitably a heated argument ensued (on the evening of 15th May) for the issue was the classic point of difference between the traditional and revolutionary military minds. Guderian must have foreseen that a

German troops cross the Meuse in a rubber boat

disagreement was bound to arise. Indeed, he had been having arguments of this sort ever since he conducted his first map battle with tanks. Perhaps because his answers were so well-rehearsed, he won Kleist round, at least to the extent of a twenty-four hour continuation.

Next day Guderian's leading tanks made forty miles, and established contact with elements of the neighbouring panzer corps, Reinhardt's. They met some brave opposition, but it struck Guderian as pretty *ad hoc*, an impression confirmed by the tone of an order from the French commander-in-chief, Gamelin, captured during the day – 'The torrent of German tanks must finally be stopped'– which suggested that Gamelin no longer believed it possible.

Guderian therefore prepared to press the advance next morning. No sooner had it begun, however, than he was ordered to halt and report personally to Kleist at a designated landing strip.

Left: Guderian in conversation with officers *Above:* General von Rundstedt

There his furiously angry senior accused him of insubordination and took Guderian at his word when the latter offered his resignation.

Guderian pretends in his memoirs to a cool indifference to the personal implications of this relief, but he reveals nevertheless that he took care that word of it should reach Rundstedt, no doubt expecting that his allies at Army Group Headquarters would rescue him from the consequences of his intemperance. And so they did – but not without making it clear that he had broken an order from OKH (the High Command of the Army) and that he must henceforth obey it.

Though Guderian must have been chastened by this reproof he had a firm intellectual conviction that he was right and his superiors were wrong. So, leaving a telephone wire from his corps headquarters (which he had been forbidden to move) to his advanced headquarters, so that neither OKH nor OKW (Wehrmacht High Command) could monitor his orders, he left for the front, intending to put the widest interpretation he could on OKH's grudging agreement that he might continue a 'reconnaissance in force'.

This reconnaissance was to prove a remarkably intrusive one. On 18th May the 2nd Panzer Division reached St Quentin on the eastern edge of the old Somme battlefield – roughly the point from which the Germans began their attack of 21st March 1918 – and the following evening had left it behind; and this despite the attempt by a whole French armoured division, commanded by de Gaulle, to halt the Germans by a flank attack. If this was not a demonstration of the extent to which armour had transformed warfare, what else was needed?

The following evening, one of 2nd Panzer Division's battalions reached the Channel coast. This was the cul-

The superiority of the Panzer division is not in doubt

Hitler confers outside his HQ in Belgium

mination of the Manstein Plan, as amended by Hitler and OKH. To the north of the long thin Panzer Corridor which Guderian and Reinhardt had opened stood the already disintegrating field armies of France, Belgium and Britain. To the south, still intact but without a will or mind to guide it, was the French Army Group Two.

Guderian expected – and panzer doctrine dictated – that the right course of action was next to consummate the destruction of the enemy's field armies. And during the next three days his divisions, having swung their axis through ninety degrees, proceeded to reduce the Channel ports and hem the British into an increasingly narrow corridor. On 24th May, however, Hitler issued a second and much more emphatic stop order. He was concerned at the development of the campaign on two main counts; the thinness of the Panzer Corridor which he wished to thicken up by giving time for the footslogging infantry to advance; and the increasing unsuitability of the northern French countryside for tank opera

ons. He could not yet foresee that the French would give up and, expecting a hard battle once he turned southwards, wished to preserve his armoured strength for it. So, to Guderian's frustration, the next thirty-six hours were spent in inactivity, hours from which the British profited to strengthen the perimeter defences of Dunkirk and evacuate much of their army.

The final stages of the campaign, when Hitler turned the armies southward and ordered the annihilation of all that remained of French military strength were exhilarating but not militarily taxing. Guderian was impressed to discover, by experiment with an anti-tank gun against a captured French Char B, how resistant it was to solid shot. And he reflected that, properly used, these tanks might have made the story of the break-through a quite different one. But this salutary thought came to him only ten days before the armistice and long after it had become obvious that the French were protracting a

Victorious Germans greet the announcement of the French request for an armistice

resistance which had become hopeless.

The announcement of the armistice on 22nd June found Guderian's corps on the Swiss frontier near Basle. It was not far south of the point from which it had started the campaign a month before, so that its progress, if drawn on a daily situation map, would describe an irregular semi-circle. This was the manoeuvre which Schlieffen had planned for the German army forty years before – just as the breakthrough to the channel was the manoeuvre which Ludendorff had planned for it in 1918. The almost contemptuous ease with which the panzers had brought off both enterprises justified all the claims which Guderian had been making for the new arm since he conceived its creation in the early nineteen-thirties.

But things would never be so easy again.

Into Russia

Guderian's armour advances into Russia at the opening of 'Barbarossa'

The laurels of victory fell thick on the German army after 22nd June 1940 Hitler resisted the temptation to parade the conquerors down the Champs Elysées but, in his own capital lavished rewards and decorations on his generals. Twelve were immediately promoted field-marshal (only five soldiers had been so promoted during the whole of the First World War) and at the same ceremony on 19th July at the Kroll Opera House, temporary home of the Reichstag Guderian and the other two Panzer Corps commanders were promoted colonel-general. It was the highest rank he was ever to hold – an interesting comment on the pattern of the relationship which was to develop between him and the Führer, in view of the fact that his most senior appointments were still ahead of him.

In the meantime his field appointment disappeared; the Panzer Group, into which XIX Corps had been transformed in the last stages of the campaign, being dissolved immediately afterwards. Guderian's responsibility contracted to that of raising and training some new panzer and motorised divisions. For while Hitler proceeded with a partial demobilisation of the war-raised infantry – public testimony of his confidence in the completeness of the victory he had won – he embarked on an expansion of the *Panzertruppen*. The number of panzer divisions was exactly doubled – from ten to twenty (the four unsatisfactory Light Divisions had been re-equipped and re-numbered as Panzer Divisions 6 to 9 immediately after the Polish campaign). But, as Guderian acidly recalls, this did not amount to a doubling of the tank strength of the army, since the older panzer divisions were simply robbed of half their vehicles to equip the new. And though this method of raising new formations is standard practice it is reputable only if the transfusion is replaced. But that Hitler did not have done; worse, the practice was to become a habit with

Char B tank captured by the Germans

him, so that the tank strength of his panzer divisions was to suffer a progressive decline throughout the war. Moreover, since he simultaneously doubled the number of motorised divisions, he badly over-taxed the output of the German automobile industry, which had to be supplemented with a great deal of captured equipment. Some of this proved excellent – for instance the confiscated Czech T35 and T38 tanks in the Polish and French campaigns. But a good deal of it was obsolete and the resulting general lack of standardisation made the maintenance and re-supply of German mobile formations much more difficult than it should have been.

On the other hand, the first panzer divisions had perhaps been tank-heavy – and tank-heavy with tanks which were individually too light. It was not therefore in principle a bad thing to redistribute the armour among a larger number of formations,

since this would increase the strength of the motorised infantry (by doubling the number of panzer Rifle Regiments – a trend of which Guderian approved). Moreover, he was at last able to say goodbye to the Panzer I and II models; henceforth the panzer divisions would be equipped exclusively with Panzer IIIs and IVs. The latter, it is true, were still mostly armed with the short, low-velocity 75mm, which was really an infantry support gun, not a tank-killer, while the Army Ordnance Officer, to Hitler's subsequent fury, decided to re-equip the Mark III with medium rather than high-velocity 50mm. Nevertheless, the twenty German panzer divisions of 1941 remained the most formidable armoured force in the world – the most experienced, the best organised, the best led, the most self-confident.

The deficiencies in Germany's military machine lay elsewhere. Some were technical and could and would be rectified, if not always in time. The current 37mm anti-tank gun was

neffective against modern armour, so
hat the heavy flak battalions of the
livisional artilleries would be con-
tantly called upon to deploy their
8mm guns in a ground role, to give
ne example. More difficult to rectify
vere deep-seated deformities in the
tructure of the Luftwaffe and the
rmy. The Luftwaffe's strategic (as
pposed to tactical) capability was
imited and its air re-supply capability
vas far too low. The army's mobility
vas also very restricted, for although
ts forty panzer and motorised div-
sions were long-striding formations,
he remaining 160 were foot-slogging
nfantry divisions, scarcely if at all
aster on the road than those of the
mperial army which had stepped off
nto Belgium in August 1914. The
ampaign in France had already
emonstrated how wide and dangerous
gap could open between a panzer
pearhead and the infantry shaft
uring a rapid thrust; over Russian
istances that gap threatened to
awn periously wide.

Panzer IV

But it was simply impossible to
motorise the bulk of the German
army. The German automobile industry lacked the factory space,
tools and manpower to equip very
many more than the total of mobile
formations already in being; indeed,
the annual tank production of 3,000
(against Russia's 12,000) was scarcely
enough to make good losses during a
tough year, and car and truck production was proportionately low. And
even if the vehicles could have been
found, the fuel could not. The German
synthetic oil industry was not yet on
stream, and the flow of imports from
Russia, the main source, could be
guaranteed only by keeping Stalin
sweet or by seizing his oil fields. And
they lay in one of the most inacces-
sible corners of Russia, in the isthmus
between the Black and Caspian seas,
beyond the Caucasus mountains.

That choice presented a strategic
dilemma, which began to nag at

Hitler as soon as the armistice with France had been signed. He was uneasily aware that his gains, having been ill-gotten, might be taken away from him by his own methods, whenever his own power weakened or his neighbours grew stronger. The wise and safe thing to do, therefore, was to destroy the last of his declared enemies, the British, and thus secure his western boundary for good. But the truth of the matter, when examined, was that the Wehrmacht lacked the means to bring off a cross-channel invasion; and it may just have been that Hitler lacked the will. In any case the failure of the Luftwaffe to win the Battle of Britain, which was evident by September 1940, prompted him to exclude it as a strategic option. He would risk leaving Britain unsubdued and hope that her American friends would confine their support of her war-effort to kind words and food parcels.

Russia's production of armour greatly exceeds that of her enemy

German 37mm anti-tank gun

But if he was to leave Britain un-beaten in the west, he could not safely preserve his non-aggression pact with Stalin in the east. The unsatisfactory state of his oil-supply situation was only one testimony of that. In the very long term he recognised that he could not endure a political equation in which Britain, Russia and America might at any time bracket their quantities against his. If he was not to cancel out Britain, then he must ensure that Russia could neither com-bine with one or other of the Western powers nor move against him inde-pendently. And if that meant attack-ing Russia, then better sooner than later.

On 5th August 1940 OKH produced, in response to a request he had made in late July, the first draft of a plan for an invasion of Russia. It was code-named 'Fritz' – later to be changed, notoriously, to 'Barbarossa' – and

General Bock

proposed an advance into Russia on
three fronts by the three familiar
Army Groups which had taken the
field in Poland and France – Leeb's,
which was to be known as Army Group
North, Bock's Group Centre and
Rundstedt's Group South. They were
to be approximately equal in infantry
strength, but Bock's Group was to
have two of the four Panzer Groups
which were to be formed for the
operation.

This allocation of the bulk of the
armour to the central front was
dictated by the peculiar geography
of western Russia, in particular the
position of the Pripet Marshes. That
virtually uncrossable swamp, a hundred miles from north to south and
300 miles from east to west, forces any
traveller from the west, whether he
comes as an enemy or merely via
Intourist, to choose either a northerly
or a southerly route; if a southerly, he

**Heinkel IIIs over the North Sea. The
Luftwaffe's failure to win the Battle
of Britain soon became evident**

	European territory ruled or dominated by Germany on 22 June 1941.
→	German advances in 1941.
┅	Front line in December 1941.
━	Line of maximum German gains.

BARENTS SEA

SWEDEN

FINLAND

NORWAY

Murmansk

WHITE SEA

Archangel

GULF OF BOTHNIA

GULF OF FINLAND

BALTIC SEA

Leningrad

Riga

EAST PRUSSIA

Kalinin

MOSCOW

Gorki

Kazan

Minsk

Smolensk

U. S. S. R.

POLAND

Pinsk

Orel

Kursk

Kiev

Saratov

HUNGARY

Kharkov

Dnepropetrovsk

RUMANIA

Odessa

Rostov

Stalingrad

Astrakhan

Sebastopol

Kerch

CASPIAN SEA

BULGARIA

BLACK SEA

Tuapse

GREECE

TURKEY

Batum

Baku

0	Miles	200
0	Kilometres	320

Advance into Russia, 1941

Stalin's strategic posture was almost as
unstable as Hitler's

will find himself crowded on his right by the Carpathian range. In short, the broad highway into Russia lies between the Pripet and the Baltic Sea – which is the way Napoleon came and the obvious route to Moscow from Poland. And faced with a choice between making the major effort in the wide-open northern arena or on the more constricted southern front – important though that was for its agricultural, manufacturing and ultimately oil-bearing regions – it was understandable that OKH should have plumped for the former.

There was however an ambiguity in the plan, which was not sorted out in the consultative phase and was to have a more and more baleful operational effect once the invasion got under way. And this concerned its long-term objects. Was the primary aim the orthodox, indeed the classic one of destroying Russia's field armies? Or was it that of winning territory, commodities, sources of supply, points of strategic importance – the Baltic ports, the industrial towns of the Donetz?

Hitler, it seems, was himself unclear. So too were his closest military advisers, though all were involved in a protracted series of debates about it. The operational generals, of whom Guderian was one, were not admitted to these uncertainties and the final

ührer Directive (No. 21) which set
ut the rationale and projected shape
f the campaign managed to suggest
hat there need be no conflict of
nterest between operational and
erritorial aims. It seems, however,
hat Hitler knew that some major re-
hinking of the campaign would be-
ome necessary within the first six
eeks; and he was certainly aware
hat Halder, Chief of Staff at OKH and
ock, commanding Army Group
entre, would then argue for a major
fort on the central front, directed at
oscow and beyond.

All this presupposed that the Wehr-
acht would make a successful break-
. to Russia's western defences.

Hitler himself was supremely confi-
dent. 'One kick at the front door,' he
told Rundstedt in the spring of 1941,
'and the whole rotten building will
crash round one's ears'. This, of
course, was chiefly a political judgement; but there was some military
foundation to it. The Red Army was
not long out of the throes of the Great
Purge, which had done for over half
its senior officers and cowed almost all
the rest. Moreover Stalin's strategic
posture was almost as unstable as
Hitler's, his territorial ambitions

**Armoured half-track troop carriers
of the Panzer-Gruppe Guderian go
forward into Russia**

Execution of Russian partisans

having carried the Red Army far to the westward of the fixed defences of the old frontier. In Poland and in the Bessarabian provinces of Rumania, it was out of touch with its familiar supply points, communications and training areas. Admittedly it had acquired depth – a valuable defensive quality – but Stalin's insistence on holding the whole of the western frontier in more or less equal strength meant that depth was not utilised for echeloning back reserves against an enemy penetration. The Red Army's defensive lay-out in the summer of 1941 was thus as badly designed as could be; thin, and lacking fixed defences, it positively invited encircling sweeps of the sort of which Germany's mobile forces were master. And the Russian armoured divisions, which might have stood back to counter such manoeuvres, had been dissolved during the Great Purge, their creator having incurred political suspicion and his creatures with him, and the component brigades had been distributed among the infantry as close support troops. And Stalin had left them there, just as if the Polish and Western campaigns had not happened.

There were grounds for optimism among the German leaders, therefore, even after Hitler's Balkan adventure, in which Guderian took no part, had delayed the opening of Barbarossa by six weeks. Guderian himself had no doubt that he could achieve his primary objective – Minsk, to be reached by an encircling drive – within five days from the start, even though it lay nearly 200 miles beyond his point of departure. He was delighted with his Panzer Group (the 2nd, which was to be renamed twice: *Panzerarmee Guderian* on 27th July and 2nd Panzer Army – as it will be referred to in this

Civilians shot by the Germans before their retreat from Rostov

ccount throughout for the sake of larity – on 5th October). It was the trongest formation he had commanded yet, though many of its nine ivisions were well known to him – the rd and 10th Panzer Divisions and the 9th Motorised Division, as well as the *rossdeutschland* Infantry Regiment. was divided into three corps – XXIV, LVI and XLVII – and included a wing f close support planes and a very rge anti-aircraft regiment. Among s formations was one of the new S field divisions – 2nd *Das Reich*, ommanded by Paul Hausser, one of ne few ex-*Reichswehr* officers to have vallowed his scruples and joined the arty's military arm.

One manifestation of Nazi intrusion ato military affairs came Guderian's ay in the last days of preparation. was OKW's directive concerning the idicial treatment of soldiers involved in excesses against the civilian opulation and prisoners; it urged scretion and leniency and Guderian cords that he accordingly ordered lat it be returned to OKW, unpublshed. The more notorious 'Commissar rder' (which laid down that political ommissars captured with Russian lits were to be shot summararily) e claims never reached him. 'No oubt', he writes, 'Army Group Centre ld already decided not to forward it'. nd it is indeed possible that the icily istocratic Bock, ex-Footguard ficer and one of the few generals illing to stand up to Hitler in an gument, had treated it with the sdain that one might expect of a russian officer of his type and generaon. But the circumstances of iderian's disclaimer require examation. *Das Reich*, which was to be sponsible for the massacre at tradour in France in July 1944, ems unlikely to have been the sort formation which would have thered to find written sanction for

the shooting of civilians at any stage. And however correct the behaviour of ordinary German army units at the outset of the Russian campaign, scruples over the mistreatment of civilians or prisoners seem to have gone by the board fairly early. Over four million prisoners were to die in German hands, the majority of them in 1941.

In June 1941, Guderian's thoughts were principally with objectives, timetabling and liaison. His most important liaison was to be with Hoth, of Panzer Group 3, with whom he was to join hands beyond Minsk in the first of the projected encirclements. Hoth's route lay north of Guderian's, whose starting point was on the Bug, at Brest-Litovsk. 'I had already captured the fortress once', Guderian wrote. Naturally he felt he knew rather more about the problems than the planners either of OKH or OKW.

Unfortunately, his superiors thought that the right way to attack the fortress was with the tanks leading. Guderian persuaded them that infantry were suited to the assault of fixed defences and that the tanks should assault on the flanks. But in order to have his way – and the extra infantry he would need – Guderian was forced to subordinate his command to Kluge, of Fourth Army, an immensely senior and very shrewd officer with whom Guderian was all too likely to fall into conflict sooner or later.

The first five days of the campaign moved, however, at too breath-taking and exhilarating a pace for there to be time for disagreements. Guderian spent 24th June, for example – and the day is not untypical – as follows: he left his headquarters at 08.25 and found some soldiers of 17th Panzer Division fighting a little battle on the main road between Rozana and Slonim, in which he joined by firing the gun of his armoured command vehicle, after which he was able to proceed. At Slonim he had a conference in the open with two of his subordinate generals, which was interrupted by

neral Hoth, Guderian's most nificant associate during rbarossa'

Russian tanks which badly wounded two of the group. Motoring back, he ran through a column of Russian infantry dismounting from their transport but his driver accelerated the vehicle out of trouble. Eventually at past ten in the evening he regained his headquarters, having been thirteen hours on the road and visited three of his fighting formations. Paperwork for next day's operations awaited him.

The 25th and 26th June were spent supervising the onward march of the panzer divisions – no need to hurry them as in Poland or France; the panzer soldiers now knew their job and Guderian's mind as well as he did. On the afternoon of 27th June the leading tanks of 17th Panzer reached the outskirts of Minsk and established touch with tanks of Hoth's Panzer Group 3. The point of Army Group Centre had thus covered 200 miles in five days and its pincers enclosed an uncounted number of Russian formations.

The next week was to be complicated for Guderian. On the one hand, with the agreement of Bock and the co-operation of Hoth, he had to prepare the ground for a further dramatic advance towards the Dneiper and Smolensk. At the same time he had to take an active part in the battle to prevent the trapped Russians from breaking out of the pockets which the German onrush had left in its rear.

There were really four of these pockets: one around Brest-Litovsk, where the fortress garrison held out for several days; one around Bialystok, where six Russian divisions were encircled; one around Volkovysk, containing another six; and the great Minsk pocket, containing fifteen divisions. Unlike the French in 1940, who had thought encirclement excuse enough to surrender, the Russians within the pockets fought hard, even after the prospects of breaking out had faded. Sometimes they managed

Infantry during the Battle of Brest-Litovsk

to break through the inner curtain of infantry, which was stretched very thin, and had to be fielded by the panzers in the outer screen.

It was frustrating for Guderian, who was burning to unshackle his panzers from these essentially static operations and lead them off in another 200 mile burst to Smolensk-Elnya-Roslavl and the crossings of the Dnieper. In the intervals of waiting, he visited his units, jockeyed them about and conferred with neighbouring commanders and superiors. He was twice taken to task by Kluge, once on 1st July for ordering 17th Panzer Division to leave the pocket and make for the Beresina crossings, the next water obstacle before the Dnieper, and again next day for failing to halt it. Guderian claims that the failure was due to a misunderstanding and that an exactly similar misunderstanding in Hoth's command

General Hoth's tanks advance while Russian prisoners make their way to the rear

as a coincidence. Kluge so little elieved him that he threatened to ave the pair court-martialled if it appened again.

This was a bad day for Guderian, hich also saw the appearance for the rst time of the Russian T-34 tank. th Panzer Division, on whose front appeared, were considerably im- essed by it, and not surprisingly, r though it usually lacked a wire- ss, was hideously uncomfortable for e crew and carried exterior petrol nks, its speed, low silhouette, thick d steeply sloped armour and power- l 76mm gun made it a better tank an any the Germans had in the ld.

Fortunately, for Guderian, the ussians had not yet produced it in mbers, nor had they yet learned to ndle it properly in action. It was t therefore to trouble Guderian

during the next stage of the advance, which began in earnest on 3rd July, following the surrender of the Russians within the Bialystok pocket. The 3rd, 4th and 18th Panzer Divisions had by that date all won themselves cross- ings over the Beresina, which it had cost Napoleon such pain to bridge from the opposite direction 130 years before. (He crossed at almost the exact point chosen by 18th Panzer.) They were now bound for the Dnieper, which leading elements reached on 5th July. On the following day the Russians counter attacked across the river in strength but were thrown back.

Guderian now had a decision to make. Evidence was growing that Russian re-inforcements were reach- ing the Dnieper front, for which they intended to fight hard. His own situa- tion was insecure. His infantry was about a fortnight behind his tanks. His supply situation was comparably tenuous. His three panzer corps were

The General during a visit to one of his units

eployed in line abreast, with their pen flanks protected by only the imsiest screens of motorised infantry nd reconnaissance troops. Should e not, rather than fight for bridge-eads from which to continue a deep dvance, construct a defensive position long the near bank and wait until he ould re-organise his base of opera-ions in orthodox fashion?

Kluge left him in no doubt as to his pinion. 'He was absolutely opposed o my decision concerning an im-iediate crossing of the Dnieper, and rdered that the operation be broken ff and the troops halted to await the rrival of the infantry. I .. defended iy plan with obstinacy', making the oint that every day's delay would llow the Russian defence to grow in trength until the ability of the in-antry, when it at last arrived, to estroy their line seemed highly

problematical. Guderian, in short, was advancing the classic panzer argument that speed is itself a weapon, and one of the most potent, for it confuses and misleads, and a confused enemy may be beaten by one much weaker in material strength. Kluge persisted, until Guderian 'told him that [his] preparations had gone too far to be cancelled . . . that the troops . . . massed on their jumping-off positions . . . could only [be kept] there for a limited length of time before the Russian air force must find and attack them'. Kluge was eventu-ally persuaded and with the words, 'Your operations always hang by a thread', he 'unwillingly gave his approval'.

The battle for Smolensk was to last for the next three weeks, and was by far the hardest episode of combat which the Panzer army had yet gone through. The advance to the Dnieper

uderian in discussion with a ommanding general in captured oslavl

113

Left: General von Kluge. *Above:* Capture of a T34 tank and its crew.
Below: Russians hasten to surrender

and the ferrying of the divisions across occupied the 10th, 11th and 12th July; Guderian himself crossed on 11th July near Tolchino, where he had temporarily had his headquarters – as had Napoleon in 1812. The advance to Smolensk took another four days, the city falling to 29th Motorised Division on 16th July.

Hoth, however, had not yet been able to fight his way to within touching distance of the city, and Guderian's Panzer army had therefore to pursue three separate aims during the next ten days. First, it had to prevent the escape southwards or eastwards of the encircled Russians; next, it had to seek touch with Hoth, fighting his way south-eastward towards it; last, and most important to Guderian, though he could not allot to the task all the forces he would have liked, it had to extend its foothold eastward,

German infantry during a lull in the fighting

towards Roslavl, which controlled the communication network of the region, and towards Elnya, from which he hoped soon to be able to jump off on the final leap towards Moscow.

Hoth did not make touch until 26th July, but the following day Guderian got Bock's permission to launch the full weight of his planned attack on Roslavl, capture of which would so much enlarge the Smolensk bridgehead, giving elbow room for the Moscow offensive. For this battle he was allotted three extra infantry corps, VII, IX and XX, and it was on this date that the title of his command was accordingly changed to *Panzer-armee Guderian*. But Guderian's mind, though actively concerned with detailed planning for the Roslavl push, was troubled by larger, if vaguer, things. There were growing signs that the direction of the war from the top

was becoming uncertain – and precisely at a moment when growing difficulties in supply and increasing enemy resistance made decisiveness essential. Ammunition for Guderian's formations was now having to be hauled nearly 300 miles by road in the divisional vehicles. Railhead itself was 450 miles back. And although the re-laying of the tracks from Russian wide to German standard gauge was proceeding apace, there was little rolling stock available as yet. But his troops desperately needed supplies. Some, of course, squandered those they got through inexperience – *Grossdeutschland* quickly learned not to expend its ammunition reserves when Guderian refused it a re-supply after some pyrotechnics had wasted all it had. But others could justify every demand. Already by 13th July, for example, 17th Panzer Division had destroyed 502 enemy tanks. Inevitably its reserves of armour-piercing shot were running low.

It may be thought surprising in the

Destroyed Russian T34 tanks

circumstances that Guderian's fear at his moment should have been that higher authority would order a halt or a diversion or a consolidation – since that might seem exactly what the situation demanded: some pause in this endless, headlong plunge into the heartland of Russia to let supplies and reinforcements catch up. But Guderian's judgement was that the German campaign, like a top which can remain upright only if it keeps spinning, would lose its momentum unless it was driven forward to Moscow. Yet evidence was accumulating that that was what was in Hitler's mind. Schmundt, his military adjutant, who came to present Guderian with Oak Leaves to his Knight's Cross hinted as much on 29th July. And on 4th August, with the Roslavl battle in full swing, Guderian heard Hitler himself announce, at a conference at Army Group Centre headquarters, that he would probably next

Russian oil transport locomotive arrives

direct the weight of the attack southwards into the Ukraine, where Rundstedt's Army Group South was not making the progress it should.

Guderian had the opportunity of arguing the case with Hitler face to face – and secured the concession that his bridgehead across the Desna at Elnya, on the Moscow highway, might be preserved against a possible resumption of the advance. 'While flying back', Guderian recalls, 'I decided in any case to make the necessary preparations for an attack on Moscow'. Roslavl having been taken on 8th August, Guderian organised a rearrangement of his forces which would allow him both to peck away at the salient on the Moscow road and enlarge his territorial holdings to the south of it.

But the period of operations which followed the Army Group Centre conference is a confusing and difficult one to describe. It has been called 'the

nineteen day interregnum', and it does indeed seem that no one was properly in charge of the war on the German side during the period, nor did anyone quite know what to do next. There was general agreement that very great damage had been done to the Russian armies: in the battle of the Minsk pockets, nearly 300,000 Russians had been made prisoner, 2,500 tanks and 1,400 guns captured or destroyed; and the encirclement battles around Smolensk had trapped another 100,000 Russians and deprived the Red Army of another 2,000 tanks and 2,000 guns. Leeb's Army Group North, though weak in armour, had made important progress, occupied most of the Baltic states and was poised to invest Leningrad. Only Rundstedt's Army Group South had fallen behind schedule in its onward march.

Nevertheless, there was a feeling widespread in the army – among field commanders, at OKH, at OKW – that things were not going right, that opportunities, perhaps unique, were passing, that time, never to be made good, was being wasted or – among the pessimists – that the Wehrmacht was being embroiled more and more deeply in a campaign which should never have been begun or should have been given less ambitious aims. Of Guderian's immediate superiors in ascending order (Kluge was no longer one), Bock at Army Group Centre was wholly for an immediate drive on Moscow, whatever the risks; Halder, Chief of Staff at OKH, was also in favour of pressing the advance, but was almost more concerned with the encroachment on his operational freedom of action by OKW; Brauchitsch, Commander-in-Chief, shared Halder's view but was too frightened of Hitler to put it to him squarely; Jodl, Chief of Staff at OKW and as shrewd a mind as any in the German army, took a radical line in private but fell in with Hitler in public; Keitel, head of OKW,

echoed whatever Hitler said, in private and public; and Hitler . . . Hitler seems simply not to have been able to make up his mind.

Guderian glimpsed this indecision in sharp focus at a conference at Army Group Centre headquarters on 23rd August, which Halder addressed. 'The latter informed us', Guderian wrote, 'that Hitler had now decided that neither the Leningrad nor the Moscow operations should be carried out, but that the immediate object should be the capture of the Ukraine and the Crimea'. In short, the effort was to be put behind Rundstedt's Army Group. All, including Halder, were dismayed by the decision and Guderian spoke so strongly against it that Bock, knowing how high he stood in the Führer's favour, suggested that he should fly back with Halder to Hitler's East Prussian headquarters and try to change his mind. They set off at once and reached Rastenburg the same evening, in time to take part in the Führer's nightly situation conference.

Guderian was met by Brauchitsch, who began disconcertingly with the words, 'I forbid you to mention the question of Moscow to the Führer. The operation to the south has been ordered. The problem now is simply how it is to be carried out. Discussion is pointless'. Guderian, with one of those flashes of insolence he could use so effectively, asked permission to fly back to the front. Brauchitsch would not agree to this. He ordered that I see Hitler and report to him on the state of my Panzer Group "but without mentioning Moscow"!'

Guderian went in – unaccompanied either by Brauchitsch or Halder, and entered a very crowded conference room. He made his report, and at the end of it Hitler, who was attended by Keitel and Jodl, asked, 'In view of their past performance, do you consider that your troops are capable of making another great effort?'.

Seeing his opening, Guderian

Above: General Jodl. *Left:* Nearly 300,000 Russians are made prisoner during the Battle of the Minsk Pocket. *Below:* General Keitel

answered, 'If the troops are given a major objective, the importance of which is apparent to every soldier, Yes.'

Hitler replied, 'You mean Moscow' – and the two men at once fell into debate. Guderian made his case – a strong one in military terms: the Russians were broken on the central front and an advance to Moscow, though it might cost the panzers the last of their strength, would finish the Russians for good, since the loss of their principal communications centre, the political 'solar plexus' of the Russian state, would deal them a material and psychological blow from which neither government, army nor people would recover. The southern operation, on the other hand, would yield only local results, and the conduct of it would exhaust his Panzer Army's fighting strength.

Hitler heard him out, and then began an exposition the keynote of which was (words Guderian heard for the first time), 'My generals know nothing of the economic aspects of this war'. He explained that the raw materials and agricultural resources of the Ukraine were essential to the prosecution of the war, and possession of the Black Sea coast, including the Crimea, vital to tha safe passage of oil supplies from the Rumanian fields. He had therefore given orders that all disposable force on the southern and south-central fronts was to rally for the encirclement of Kiev and the destruction of the Russian forces in presence there.

Guderian, noting 'for the first time a spectacle . . . which was later to become very familiar: all those present [nodding] in agreement with every sentence that Hitler uttered', perceived that no purpose would be served by making an 'angry scene with the head of the German State'. He instead accepted the redirection of the campaign and returned to his Panzer Army determined to make it work as well and as quickly as he could.

Hoth, whose leading units were even

further advanced towards Mosco than Guderian's, had also to acquiesc in a diversion, for his panzers were t be turned northwards to expedi Leeb's advance on Leningrad. N until the two Panzer Armies could l returned to Bock would he have ar hope of resuming the advance on tl central front.

Bock seems to have been fairly di pleased with Guderian when he r turned, Halder even more so. They fel it appears ,that Guderian had let tl side down and had given in to Hitle He himself took the view, with whic one must sympathise, that as the junior it was not really for him t make the case in the first plac Loyalty, which generals preach as cardinal military virtue to the soldiers, frequently does not chara terise their own relationships.

The Kiev operation, which involve a southward approach march of ov 200 miles, was to occupy Guderian f the next month. As 'battles of annih lation' go, it was to prove immensel successful, for the encircleme around Kiev yielded even more pri oners than either that of Minsk c

German possession of the Black Sea coast was vital for the safe passage of Rumanian oil supplies

molensk: perhaps over 600,000. ...uderian found the whole episode ...ustrating, however, all the more ...ecause they had now entered the ...me of the *rasputitsa* or *Schlammperiode* ...autumnal rains, which broke up the ...oads. He records, for example, taking ...en hours to cover a hundred miles on ...0th September and ten and a half to ...over eighty miles next day; both in ...he course of his interminable visita-...ons to his fighting units. On 16th ...eptember, nonetheless, his leading ...anks made contact with those of ...leist's Panzer Army, which was ...rawing the other arm of the pincer ...round the Russians in Kiev. There ...as then only the mopping-up of the ...ocket to complete, which took until ...3rd September. On that day, he was ...eleased from his duty with Rundstedt ...nd allowed to begin his regrouping ...or the drive towards Moscow, which ...itler had at last agreed, the situation ...n the other fronts being satisfactory, ...ould now follow.

There was precious little time in ...hich to conclude the 1941 campaign ...ctoriously. The first snows usually ...ll in late October; in 1812 they had not fallen until 6th November, but Napoleon had been lucky (or unlucky). On the other hand, the period until the coming of the frosts was unsuitable for movement. Guderian was therefore frantic to get his offensive under way. He was too start off from positions rather to the south of those which he had prepared at Elnya, moving from Roslava on Bryansk and Orel, where he was to close the jaws of a pincer with Second Army; Hoth, meanwhile, was to co-ordinate a similar pincer move-ment to the north with Hoepner's Panzer Army, detached from Army Group North. Bock's Army Group would then have strong armoured columns within a hundred miles of Moscow and positioned to achieve the greatest and most decisive encircle-ment of the campaign so far.

Guderian had three Panzer Corps under command for this operation: XXIV, XLVII and XLVIII. All were under strength, and though a re-inforcement of a hundred tanks arrived

General Hoepner

at the last minute only fifty were ready in time for the start. The men were desperately tired and the equipment, largely because of the incessant action of the dust, of which Guderian complains constantly in his memoirs of this period, was badly worn. But the soldiers were resolved to win. They believed that the German forces could not fail to finish off an army which had already shown by how much it was inferior to their own; perhaps, however, at the back of their minds lurked unpleasant forebodings of what a winter war might be like. Some of them, after all, were great-grandsons of the Saxons and Wurttembergers who had marched in Napoleon's Grand Army in 1812.

After a sharp fight the Panzer Army successfully broke through to the line Orel-Bryansk, destroying or driving before them very large numbers of Russians. That night, however, the first snow fell and Guderian repeated his as yet unanswered request to OKH that winter clothing be sent forward to the fighting formations. OKH, satisfied with progress both on Guderian's and on Hoth's front at Viasma, ordered

the next stage to begin, an advance t Tula, a hundred miles due south o Moscow. This was premature, how ever, Guderian recording that 'thes weeks were dominated by the mud', s that he had to get about by light air craft and his men had to struggl forward as best they could. Not unti 25th October could he regard th situation on the Orel-Bryansk fron as sufficiently cleared up for him t push on towards Tula.

The Panzer army was successful i seizing crossings over the Oka, now the last important obstacle betwee: themselves and Moscow, and o 29th October his tanks were withi two miles of Tula. But thereafte progress was to grow slower an slower. On 7th November his chie medical officer reported the firs severe cases of frost-bite and on 13t] November the temperature droppee to −13 degrees (Fahrenheit), or 4 degrees of frost. His men were stil wearing denim trousers, unless the had been able to find Russian uniforms and the tanks could only be started b lighting fires under them.

Fortunately, from a tactical poin of view, the German soldier in th front line was not called upon t attempt long-range movement, fo throughout the rest of November, th battle for Tula remained static. Bu the Russians were bringing reinforce ments to the scene and Guderian wa growing more and more worried fo his command and pessimistic abou the turn the campaign had taken. O the afternoon of 23rd November h decided to visit Bock personally an explain that he could see no way o pressing his attack forward. OKH which they jointly telephoned, in sisted that conditions at the fron were appreciated but that orders mus be carried out. Next day he sent th

During the first winter on the Western Front sheepskin coats were issued. Inadequate winter clothing during the Russian campaign caused major problems for the German forces

OKH liaison officer from his own headquarters back to emphasise the
difficulties, but with similar lack of
effect. Things were now getting
desperate, and not only on Guderian's
front. On 28th November word came of
the Russians' first real success of the
war – the recapture of Rostov from
Army Group South. On the night of
5th/6th December, Hoepner's Fourth
Panzer Army, only twenty miles
away from Moscow in the north, was
compelled to abandon its offensive.
And at the same time Guderian himself came to that decision also.

For the next three weeks, while he
beat off one Russian attack after
another around Tula, giving ground
here and there when he had to, he
bombarded higher authority with
requests to be allowed to make a
proper withdrawal to a more defens-

**The Russian counter-offensive forces
the German army to withdraw from
the Moscow region**

Russian reinforcements leaving Moscow for the front, 1941

ible line, speaking to Bock, Schmundt, Hitler's adjutant and eventually to Hitler himself. Eventually, on 17th December he got permission to fly once again to Rastenburg and report personally to the Führer. The conference took place on 20th December, lasted five hours, and ended in what Guderian described as 'complete failure'. Hitler would not hear of a large-scale withdrawal. He was sure it would bring about a disaster of the sort which had overtaken Napoleon.

Next day, therefore, he returned to his headquarters with a heavy heart. It was now only a matter of time before it came to a breach between him and his superiors. Bock, who had shared his viewpoint despite many disagreements, had been replaced by his old enemy Kluge on 20th December. On 26th December, following yet another argument about withdrawal, the new Army Group Commander dismissed him.

The supreme command

Following defeat in the Battle of Moscow Hitler dismisses a number of his generals, amongst them Guderian

Guderian was but one among many generals to go under the axe following the defeat in the Battle of Moscow. Brauchitsch, Commander-in-Chief, was the most prominent victim, and his office now passed to Hitler, who thus became executive as well as titular head of the army. Bock had gone, to be replaced by the more pliant Kluge, Leeb went in early January, Rundstedt had a polite disagreement with Hitler and was transferred to the west: thus all three Army Group Commanders – who as *Obergruppen* commanders had held their posts since 1938 – disappeared together. Hoepner, to whose handling of his Panzer Army Hitler had taken strong exception,

was cashiered. Thirty-five corps or divisional commanders were also dismissed. Guderian could not therefore claim to have been singled out for disfavour.

Indeed, in view of his habit of baiting the Führer face to face as at Rastenburg or, failing that, over the long-distance telephone, it is surprising that Hitler let him down as lightly as he did. But Hitler respected Guderian. He may even rather have liked him. And he was honest enough a strategist, at least at this stage of the war, to recognise that Guderian might have been right during the crucial days of indecision in July and August. Intelligence was accumulating to show,

... e of the many armoured vehicles lost ...ring the battle

... Guderian had then insisted, that ...e Russians, though still numerous, ...ere immobile, paralysed, and that ...ldly handled tank forces could well ...ve infiltrated between the stranded ...d bleeding hulks of their field armies ...strike a fatal blow at Moscow.

...But those were profitless regrets. ...uderian was to nurse them – and his ...rd feelings at the way he had been ...eated – throughout the campaigning

...e German retreat after the ...successful attempt to capture the ...ssian capital

season of 1942 and into 1943. These were critical and ultimately desperate months for the German army and nation. During the winter of 1941–2, the German army in Russia (the *Ostheer*) suffered an ordeal which in its intensity if not totality is comparable to that undergone by Napoleon's Grand Army in 1812. Up to the end of November 1941 it had suffered about 700,000 casualties, of which 200,000 were fatal; in the next four months, although fatal casualties were lower, at 100,000, there were 260,000 wounded, a quarter of a million frost-bite cases and another quarter of a million sick. The total deficiency for the period of the Russian

counter-offensive was 900,000 and by April over 600,000 had yet to be replaced. A quarter of a million horses, half those which had been brought to Russia, had been lost, with a serious effect on the army's capacity to manoeuvre, and it had also lost 2,300 armoured vehicles and was short of 2,000 guns and 7,000 anti-tank guns.

Despite this appalling toll, the Germans were able to conduct an orderly retreat wherever they were forced to, to hold the line elsewhere, and in the spring to resume the offensive with an advance which, in its pace and depth, seemed to threaten Russia with defeat even more certainly than the great *blitzkrieg* of 1941 had

done. This time the sweeping capture of ground were made on the souther front, where Rundstedt's Army Grou had been so slow to make progress i 1941. By August 1942, Army Group (part of the former Group South) ha reached the Volga, after an advanc of 300 miles and Army Group A (th other part of Group South) had i front on the crests of the Caucasu mountains, beyond which lay th weakly-defended oil fields.

Throughout this period of fres triumphs, Guderian led the life of retired and none too fit warrior. E was shunned by the official ar military hierarchy and moved fro Berlin in March 1942 in order to nur

therefore, that on 17th February 1943 he was ordered to report to Hitler at his field headquarters at Vinnintsa in the Ukraine. When he arrived, Schmundt, the Führer's military adjutant, explained to him that the armoured force as a whole was in a parlous condition, both from the morale and the equipment points of view, the General Staff and the Armaments Ministry, which was responsible for development of new tanks, were at odds and that the men of the panzer units had lost confidence in their leadership. Hitler had therefore decided to centralise all training and equipment responsibilities and invest them in a single officer – his choice was Guderian.

Guderian was attracted by the challenge of this post, but was concerned that he should have full authority. He therefore made certain conditions, principally that he report directly to Hitler, not to the Chief of Staff, that he have authority over Waffen SS and Luftwaffe armour and that he treat on terms of equality with the Armament Ministry and the Ordnance Office.

Hitler sent word that he accepted these conditions and Guderian was brought in to see him. The meeting was cordial. Hitler knew how to charm when he wanted to and his opening words were calculated to disarm: 'Since 1941 our ways have parted. There were numerous misunderstandings ... which I much regret. I need you.' Napoleon could scarcely have done it better. Guderian, at any rate, felt that there had been a genuine reconciliation and set off to tackle his new task with enthusiasm.

He would need a stout heart. Germany had undergone, in the winter of 1942, a genuine military disaster, beside which the setbacks of the Battle of Moscow paled. Stalingrad had removed a whole army from its order of battle; the soldiers and equipment of twenty divisions had been

heart, which was betraying symptoms of the strain he had been under the past two and a half years. He s now thinking of buying a small operty in south Germany to which might eventually retire and when September it was made clear to n, following the dismissal of a ggestion by Rommel that Guderian ght deputise for him during his sence from the Western Desert, that would never be employed again, he de firm plans to settle down in the intry. His heart condition suddenly w worse, he suffered a collapse and ring the winter of 1942–3 he only wly recovered his strength.

t was to his complete surprise,

After the Battle of Stalingrad the German army's sense of invincibility was broken

The famous Tiger tank

lost and the Wehrmacht's sense of invincibility had been broken, never to be restored. The Russians, moreover, had begun to demonstrate a frightening superiority in armoured equipment and expertise in the handling of armoured formations on the field of battle. The T-34, in production at the rate apparently of hundreds a week, could outgun and outmanoeuvre the Panzer IV wherever the two tanks met, and it was only the individual skills of the German tank crews and commanders which still allowed the Germans to meet the Russians on more or less equal terms. The need for better tanks and replacement crews to man them was a burning priority.

When Guderian turned to examine the situation he found it a dispiriting one. In November 1941 he had been visited at his headquarters by experts from the Army Ordnance Office on a tour of inspection of panzer units in Russia. As a result of their findings it was decided to produce two new tanks – a superheavy which was to become famous as the Tiger and a medium,

which was to answer the T-34 and was eventually called the Panther. Their report was accepted at a Führer conference in January 1943, where tank production targets were set at 600 a month. It was also decided very greatly to increase the production of what the Germans called assault guns – effectually tank guns mounted on armoured but turretless tracked chassis. They were to become standard equipment in the anti-tank battalions of the panzer divisions and to provide the armoured element in the motorised divisions (soon to be named *panzergrenadier* divisions). The Western Allies in particular were to develop a healthy respect for the assault gun. But Guderian regarded it as an essentially defensive weapon, since it was at a disadvantage in a tank-to-tank engagement.

Guderian was therefore dismayed to discover, on taking up his duties, that monthly production figures for tanks and assault guns were running about equal: some hundred Panzer IVs and

Panzergrenadier troops at a tank training school

25 Tigers were being turned out by the factories, but so also were a hundred assault guns, while the obsolescent Panzer III, which was being produced at about a hundred a month, was to be discontinued in favour of yet more assault gun production. The advantage of the assault gun from the bureaucratic and industrial point of view was that, since it lacked a turret and the complicated and expensive traversing gear which went with it, it could be produced more quickly and cheaply than a tank of equivalent gun-power. The logic of this approach led towards the suppression of all tanks of similar gun-power to assault-guns. And indeed, when Guderian took office, the General Staff had just suggested that production of the last pre-war tank – the Panzer IV – should stop and only Tigers and Panthers be produced. Since the Panther was still

in the prototype stage, German tank production would in that case have been limited to twenty-five Tigers a month.

Guderian had been recalled precisely in order to avert proposals of that sort being made. In fact it was never accepted; but nonetheless he had a great deal of obscurantism against which to struggle. A typical example was the attitude of the Inspectorate of Artillery, which managed by administrative sleight of hand to get responsibility for all assault-guns withheld from Guderian – their unspoken reason being that, since this was the last arm in which artillery-men could win the Knight's Cross, they wanted sole authority over the handling of this prestigious branch. Fortunately, Guderian was able to establish a warm personal and sound working relationship with Speer, the young architect whom Hitler had recently appointed Minister of Armaments, one of his best ministerial choices. Between them, they were very significantly to raise German armoured vehicle production figures. In May 1943 they were able to tell Hitler that tank production for that month would reach over 300, thrice that of the end of the previous year.

It cannot be pretended, however, that Guderian's appointment as Inspector-General was a happy or a rewarding period for him. His independence was not full enough for him to achieve the results he wanted, but such independence as he had acquired was so resented by the army bureaucracy that good relations between his small staff and that of OKH or other authorities was ruled out. Moreover, though Hitler would listen to his advice, and listen a good deal more patiently than he would to that of other generals, he would not take it. And as Hitler was now more and more assuming direct control of operations, this meant that Guderian had no real

say, though he itched to have, in the running of the war. OKW, Hitler's personal headquarters which was responsible for the conduct of all operations outside Russia, was closed to him – as it was to all 'non-OKW' officers. OKH, which ran the Russian campaign on a day-to-day basis but with Hitler taking the major strategic decisions, was hostile to his views on principle. Thus it was that even on an issue where Hitler kept an open mind (the decision for or against the great Summer offensive of 1943 at Kursk – codenamed 'Citadel' – being the outstanding example), the wall-like opposition of the Army General Staff to his reasoned criticism of their plans produced a majority vote to which Hitler deferred.

And Hitler, moreover, was given when he felt like it to interfering even within Guderian's special sphere of panzer organisation and training. A new Panzer Division, the 25th, which Guderian had been able to set up by dint of a great deal of borrowing and scraping together of equipment, was transferred from Norway, where it was just learning the ropes of armoured warfare, to France, where it was ordered to hand over most of its equipment to another newly formed division bound for Russia. Shortly afterwards it too was dispatched to the eastern front on Hitler's orders, though still only half-trained and now without most of its armoured vehicles. Nevertheless it was thrown into battle as if it were a fully up-to-strength panzer formation and, when almost destroyed in the subsequent débacle, its commander was dismissed in disgrace.

Guderian watched, more and more disheartened, as one failure followed another during the course of 1943 and early 1944: the disastrous setback at Kursk, the breakthrough into the Ukraine, the relief of Leningrad, the loss of the Crimea. He was moreover becoming more and more concerned by the threat of invasion in the west, which Hitler thought of countering

Hitler with Albert Speer, Minister of Armaments

Russian farm women help build defence lines in preparation for the battle of Kursk

only by the building of larger and more costly fortifications. Guderian wanted to increase the number of mobile formations available to meet the British and American armies, which were supplied with fighting vehicles of all sorts on a scale to make a German tank commander's mouth water, and he was particularly anxious to add to the numbers of mobile, armoured anti-aircraft guns, since he feared Allied air power and knew that the Luftwaffe would not be able to match it in the skies.

On that score, his worst anxieties were to be realised, for within a few days of the Allies landing in Normandy in June 1944 the panzer divisions of the German army of the west were prevented from moving in

Capture of German troops in the Ukraine

German defeat at Kursk

daylight outside the immediate combat zone. Worse still, because the Allied air forces absolutely interdicted movement on the railways, the infantry formations which should have been able to make their way forward to the relief of the panzer divisions, which had been committed in the first crisis, were unable to get up to the battle. Guderian had therefore to watch, helpless with frustration, as one after another of his cherished formations went down under the hammer of Allied material superiority. For none did he feel as much as *Panzer Lehr* Division, the strongest in the German army, which he himself had formed from the precious and elite armoured training units of the German army. It was to be almost completely destroyed in the fighting on the British sector of the bridgehead and the remnant to be sent limping away from the battlefield even before the Normandy battle was over.

By then Germany was to have suffered a disaster of unsurpassed magnitude on the eastern front, one so large that it has come to be known simply as The Destruction of Army Group Centre. It was to send the German armies reeling back out of western Russia and the broken formations of the centre were to be halted only after a retreat of 200 miles. That the line could be stabilised at all was due to the over-extension of the Russians' own services of supply, though also to a remarkable and very ruthless display of leadership by one of Guderian's old panzer division commanders, Field-Marshal Model.

While Germany was suffering military defeat on both major fronts, the opposition to Hitler's leadership within the army, which had remained mute and inactive during the years of victory, suddenly erupted. A bomb, placed under the map table at Hitler's headquarters at Rastenberg during the mid-day conference by the chief of staff of the Home Army, Colonel Stauffenberg, only narrowly failed to kill the Führer. A simultaneous attempt to seize the organs of government in Berlin was defeated when Goebbels managed to get a message through from Rastenberg to the commander of the Berlin guard battalion, who proved to be loyal. Interrogations, which began at once,

evealed widespread army complicity
in the plot. A number of officers were
later executed for their parts, or
alleged parts, in it. A great many
more were immediately dismissed.
Among them was the Chief of Staff,
Zeitzler.

Guderian insists that he knew
nothing of the plot until he got word
by telephone on the evening of 20th
July that he was to fly to Rastenberg
next day to replace Zeitzler. This
may be true. On the one hand, the
plot – or a plot – had been brewing for
years and almost every senior officer
in the army had heard rumours of it;
the conference at Bock's headquarters
attended by Guderian on 4th August,
'41, at which Hitler had first revealed
his intention of swinging away from
Moscow, had been selected by some
conspirators as a moment when he
might have been kidnapped. But their
nerve had failed. Had Guderian, who
was in many ways so close to Bock,
not been aware of what was afoot?
Perhaps not. For the conspirators
may very well have marked Guderian
down as an unknown quantity on
their lists of 'for' and 'against'. He
had, after all, been very rapidly
promoted by Hitler, been intimate
with him, been regarded as one of his
favourite generals. Since we cannot
know one way or the other, Guderian's
word ought to stand.

He was completely unprepared for
the responsiblities that Zeitzler's
removal now thrust upon him, all
the more so in that he had at once to
undertake a major re-organisation of
the General Staff. OKH, he discovered,
was in the process of being moved back
to Zossen, near Berlin. He believed that
it had to be near Hitler and OKW if
it was to work efficiently and so had
to get it relocated at Rastenberg. He
had also to find many new staff officers
many of those previously in post
having been removed for suspicion
of complicity in the plot; at least one
had committed suicide.

Meanwhile, Guderian found himself
involved in a highly distasteful duty.

In order to proceed in the civil courts
against the conspirators, the Gestapo
had first to secure the dismissal of the
suspected officers from the army.
Guderian was therefore obliged to
attend meetings of a specially constituted Court of Honour at which
these men were examined. Naturally,
he did the best he could to protect
them against the consequences of
the damaging disclosures which so
many of them made before it.

The military situation which he
inherited was a profoundly alarming
one. In the west, the Allies had
recently succeeded in breaking clean
out of their bridgehead, of encircling
the German armies which Hitler had
ordered to counterattack them, and
of destroying all but a handful of the
fifty divisions in Normandy. Their
commander, Guderian's old enemy
Kluge, incurred suspicion of treason
in Hitler's eyes and committed suicide
on being summoned to the Führer's
headquarters. He was to be replaced
by Model, the miracle-worker from
the eastern front, three weeks after
Guderian took office. But there were
no miracles to be worked on the
western front, and the first weeks of
Model's command saw nothing but a
long withdrawal – but nonetheless an
orderly one – into the Low Countries.

On the eastern front, there was a
temporary lull at the end of July on
the most threatening sector; that
leading through Poland and Prussia
to Berlin. Stalin had decided to exert
pressure on the more vulnerable and
politically desirable Balkans and
during the course of August and
September was to organise offensives
which won him wide tracts of territory
in Rumania, Bulgaria and Hungary.
The Rumanian and Bulgarian governments, moreover, took this as the
moment to change sides – though too
belatedly to retain power themselves.

Although these advances did not
threaten German territory in the way
that the great breakthrough into
Poland in June had done, their potential effect on Germany's capacity to

US troops land in France, June 1944

General Model

wage war was very grave. The loss of Rumania meant also the loss of her oil-fields. And as German synthetic oil production was now under concentrated attack by the Allied air-forces, some supply of natural oil was essential to Germany. Possession of the Hungarian fields around Lake Balaton, small though they were, thus suddenly acquired a special significance.

Three other problems, among the multitude which beset Germany in the late summer of 1944, particularly oppressed Guderian. One was the danger of encirclement threatening Schoerner's Army Group North in Estonia (Kurland); the second was the need to provide arms for the fortifications and local civilian defence forces in eastern Germany; the third was to amass a new reserve for the field army and see that it was committed at the right time in the right place.

The question of the defence of the eastern provinces was settled in a fashion very much against Guderian's better judgement. He wanted to create out of the old Brownshirt movement a local home guard under army control. He also wanted to withdraw from store the great stocks of captured foreign weapons and install them in the forts of Prussia and Silesia. The Party, however, holding itself in charge of the Brownshirts insisted on the home guard (*Volksturm*) they provided being subjected to Party control and on its being raised throughout Germany, with consequent wasteful dispersion of the available arms. The captured weapons, too, were misused, being sent to the west instead of the east.

It was there too that Hitler planned to use the reserve for the field army. The commander of home forces had had some considerable success in raising new divisions and Guderian was counting on these to prop up the eastern front when the Russians renewed their offensive towards Berlin which could not be long delayed. He was very distressed, therefore to discover in the early autumn that Hitler was thinking of employing them in the west, in pursuit of a political calculation of his that a major setback to the Western Allies would cause them to sue for a separate peace.

His fears for the safety of Army Group North in Kurland were part and parcel with those he felt for the integrity of the eastern front as a whole. Hitler, now as always, resolutely opposed any voluntary surrender of ground there, whatever the arguments for shortening the front, evacuating useless salients and releasing formations to create a reserve. Undoubtedly he had been right in the past to forbid withdrawals under pressure which experience showed the Germans could weather. He was also probably right now to turn down some of Guderian's suggestions for withdrawals which would have shortened the eastern front, since there was virtually no ground which could be given up without reducing the defe ive buffer. But Hitler's determination to hang on to Kurland did not then make sense, nor does it now, and one must sympathise with Guderian's frustrated bewilderment in trying to make him change his mind.

The argument was to drag on to the end of Guderian's tenure of office, by which time Army Group North had been completely surrounded and could plan no useful part in operations at all. In the meantime, Hitler's policy had deprived the *Ostheer* of the use of nineteen infantry and five panzer divisions.

Hitler, throughout the autumn, would lend only half an ear to Guderian's expressions of fear for the eastern front. He was obsessed with his coming 'masterstroke' in the west and resisted every effort by the field commanders nominated to carry out to reduce it in scope. He was for a 'big solution' which, if successful, would carry the Sixth Panzer Army to Antwerp, cut the British off from the Americans – as Guderian had cut the British off from the French in 1940 – and shock the two western powers into making a separate peace.

The attack began on 16th December, employing almost all the fresh formations which the home forces command had been able to raise during the autumn. At first it made good progress having taken the Americans badly by surprise and having been launched during weather which made flying impossible and so deprived the Allies of the advantage which their air superiority gave them. By 23rd December, however, the attack had fallen so far behind schedule that it was clear that the offensive had failed. It had done so at the irredeemable cost of the last fresh panzer divisions in the German army.

In the east, Guderian had now only twelve panzer divisions to bolster up a front over 700 miles long. To assemble even that number in reserve had been a considerable achievement, for which Hitler in one of his now very rare

The Chief of Staff, Zietzler, whom Guderian replaced after the former's dismissal

flashes of gratitude, thanked Guderian. 'The eastern front', he said 'has never before possessed such a strong reserve.'

'The eastern front', Guderian answered, 'is like a house of cards. If the front is broken through at one small point, the house will collapse'. He calculated that the Russians enjoyed a superiority over the Germans of eleven to one in infantry, seven to one in tanks, twenty to one in guns and twenty to one in the air. They were continuing to make progress on the Balkan front, having encircled Budapest, the capital of Hungary, by 24th December and having also reached Lake Balaton. He expected them to renew their attack across the Vistula, into German territory, on 12th January.

His calculation was exactly accurate. On that day, very large Russian forces, perhaps seventy divisions strong, broke out of the bridgehead across the Vistula at Baranov in southern Poland and headed towards

Bormann consults with Göring in the devastated map-room at Rastenberg

Silesia. At the same time, other Russian armies crossed the Narev and advanced on East Prussia and Pomerania. On 20th January, 'the army set foot on German soil. This was the beginning of the last act'.

There was now little that Guderian could do to influence the way that it was played out. He had, for one thing, very little time in each day in which to do his staff work, for Hitler expect-

ed him to be present at each of his daily conferences which, as the news from the front grew worse, took up more and more time. He estimated that with travelling between OKH at Zossen, to which it had now returned and the Chancellery bunker in Berlin eight or nine hours were expended on these briefings. The freedom to visit units at the front was now almost completely curtailed, and was further hampered by the Allied air offensive which was causing widespread destruction to the German domestic mmunications network.

Guderian did manage to see a number of influential figures in the party and government, for he was now convinced that Germany must come to terms with her enemies before she was completely overwhelmed. But he could find no one who, even at this stage, was prepared to risk the consequences should the news of their diplomatic efforts reach Hitler's ear. Guderian himself had abandoned cares for his own safety. He had never been hesitant in standing up to Hitler, and some extraordinary scenes had resulted between them as a result. Moreover his health had now begun to suffer a renewed setback because of the strain under which he was living and working, which further reduced his sense of having anything to lose. Thus emboldened, he was able to achieve one or two minor alleviations of the agony the German army was suffering. In early March, he prevailed upon Himmler, who was acting quite, unsuitably, as commander of Army Group Vistula, besides retaining all his responsibilities for intelligence and repression, to surrender his command to a qualified soldier. He also did what he could to help Speer, the armaments minister, in his efforts to preserve, in the face of Hitler's direct order to the contrary, as much as possible of Germany's industrial plant and communications infrastructure.

The growing tide of military setbacks which he had to discuss with Hitler each day, however, were undermining his position as Chief of Staff. They would have made the position of any officer impossible, unless he was craven enough to agree that he and not Hitler was ultimately responsible for the pass to which the Führer's strategy had brought Germany. But this Guderian would not do. Nor would he allow Hitler to vent his fury and frustration on subordinates who happened to be unfortunate enough to command in areas where disasters occurred. On 21st March Hitler told him that he ought to take sick leave –

a hint that their relationship was nearing breaking-point. Guderian answered quite sincerely that there was no one available to replace him at OKH, his two immediate juniors both having been recently wounded, one in a heavy Allied air attack on Zossen, in which Guderian himself had narrowly escaped injury. A week later, during the course of another argument in which he sought to protect a field commander from some unjustifiable allegation of negligence, Guderian was abruptly told by Hitler that he must immediately go on six weeks' sick leave. For form's sake, he waited until the end of the conference, and then left Berlin to re-join the Armoured Troops Inspectorate staff, of which he remained head. There, in the Tyrol, he waited for the end of the war and on 10th May was taken prisoner by the American army.

Like all the leading German generals who survived, Guderian was to spend a considerable length of time in Allied captivity. Unlike many, however, he was not arraigned for war crimes and he was eventually released into a quiet retirement. He died in 1953.

How are we to assess Guderian's place among the great generals of the twentieth century? It is perhaps most meaningful to look at him first as a German soldier rather than as a tank pioneer or a 'panzer leader'. For, to German eyes, the most obvious thing about him was the conventionality of his background and the extent to which he had followed, at least up until 1940, an orthodox career. He was, first of all, a Prussian and, though his Prussianism comes out only by implication in what he has to say about himself, the arena of many of his achievements lay in the traditional Prussian zone for feats of arms – that between the Oder and the Memel. He had been born there, in a town which he was to see pass to Poland in the years of German humiliation after 1918 and which he was to see again at the moment of its recapture in 1939.

Above: German troops with a captured Russian T34 in a Rumanian town before th
loss of Rumania to the Red Army. *Below:* Fighting in Warsaw during the Russian
breakthrough into Poland

Nowhere does Guderian suggest that the loss of the West Prussian provinces was anything but a regret to him or their recapture anything but a consolation. And although he had not taken part in the German campaign in Russia during the First World War, which brought the German army its most impressive list of victories, little known as they are in the west, his service on the Baltic coast in the war's immediate aftermath was an experience common to many of the regular officers who were to make their careers in the 100,000 army and later rise to senior rank in the Wehrmacht. That sequence of events, which appears to a western observer to be a discontinuous collection of episodes, many of them transpiring on

Hitler's planned 'masterstroke' to attack Belgium is launched, December 1944

NORTH SEA

SWEDEN

LITH.

BALTIC SEA

DENMARK

Kiel Canal

Kiel

Rostock

Königsberg

Danzig

EAST PRUSSIA

HOLLAND

Lübeck

Elbe

Hamburg

Lüneburg

Bremen

Hanover

Brunswick

Stettin

Oder

Kolberg

Vistula

POLAND

Warsaw

Arnhem

BELG.-LUX.

Cologne

Kassel

BERLIN

Oder

Leipzig

Neisse

Lodz

Dresden

GERMANY

Frankfurt

Main

CZECHOSLOVAKIA

Prague

Cracow

Vistula

FRANCE

Nuremberg

Stuttgart

Rhine

Berchtesgaden

Danube

Brünn

Salzburg

Vienna

SWITZERLAND

BRENNER PASS

AUSTRIA

HUNGARY

Budapest

Danube

FRANCE

Milan

Po

Venice

Zagreb

YUGOSLAVIA

Belgrade

Turin

Genoa

ADRIATIC SEA

Florence

ITALY

◀	Main Allied advances.
───	The battlefronts on 27 January 1945.
▄▄▄	The battlefronts on 8 May 1945.

0 Miles 100
0 Kilometres 160

Reichsführer SS Himmler visiting a
Waffen SS unit on his 44th birthday,
7th October 1944

non-German soil, looks quite different
to Germans of Guderian's background,
class and profession. To them, the
most enduring and important factor
in the history of that Baltic coast-line
and its hinterland is the Prussian
presence, which brought civilisation
and Christianity to the region and
ensured order, government and trade
for 500 years. Hence the untroubled
tone of Guderian's description of the
Polish blitzkrieg of 1939 – viewed by
the west as the unjust destruction of
a national and sovereign state, but
by Prussian military professionals as
the breaking of a purely arbitrary rearrangement of the political geography of the area imposed by the
western powers for their own selfish
strategic ends.

To turn to Guderian's achievement
as a tank pioneer. He was not among
the very small group of German
officers who had had experience o
tanks during the fighting on th
western front. He did not in fact se
the inside of a tank until several year
after the war was over. His earl
thinking and writing about tan
warfare had a purely theoretical basi
and grew out of his study of supply an
transport problems. It is all the mor
remarkable therefore that he shoul
have reached the very sound con
clusions that he did, and that on thos
conclusions he should have built s
creatively. He was not alone amon
European soldiers of his generation t
glimpse that the tank offered a mean
of transforming warfare in the machin
age. Liddell Hart and Fuller in England
de Gaulle in France, Tukhachevsk
in Russia were preaching the sam
message. But of these perhaps onl
Liddell Hart saw in more or less exac
fashion how it was that tank force
should be organised. Fuller, for all th
brilliance of his mind and pen, un
doubtedly overestimated the impor
tance of the tank itself, for which h

Guderian with Liddell Hart in 1950

vished to claim almost magical powers. De Gaulle, on the other hand, though he demanded a major expansion of the tank complement of the French army, does not seem to have been altogether clear about what he would have done with it if granted it. Both Liddell Hart and Guderian, however, the former undoubtedly influencing the latter but by no means forming his mind completely, saw that the tank's value lay in its combination with conventional weapons and arms of the service, organised into large, mobile formations. And Guderian saw even more clearly than Liddell Hart that a vital element in that combination would be provided by air power. In a real sense, Guderian is the first protagonist of effective land-air operations, experience in the organisation of which he had had, in a training context, as early as 1924. Moreover, Guderian never swerved from his belief in the battle-winning power of armour–air formations, as Liddell Hart did in the year before the

Second World War. Indeed, Guderian's confidence in the weapon was sustained and continued to grow throughout all the nerve-wracking days of the Polish, French and early Russian campaigns.

Which leads one to ask how good he was as a commander of troops in the field. For someone whose first extended period of command authority was as commander of a Panzer Corps, Guderian showed an astonishingly sure touch. Perhaps he was not really tested during the Polish campaign, the powers of resistance of the Polish army being as unequal to the German as they were. But he showed from the outset that readiness to expose himself to danger, to set a personal example, to go and see for himself, to judge by his own senses the intensity and pattern of the fighting and the reaction to it of the men under his command, which were to make him such an outstandlingly inspiring leader and uncannily accurate forecaster of events and master of timing. He was to display all these qualities to full effect

both during the overthrow of the Western Allies in 1940 and during the blitzkrieg in Russia in 1941. Nor, despite his peripatetic style of command, did he ever fall into the trap of losing sight of the whole picture in whatever zone he was responsible for. 'Forward control', of which he was a pioneer, did mean control to him, even if he spent a great deal of time forward even of his advanced headquarters. It was here that his long training as a signal officer stood him in such stead; and indeed, one might argue that if Guderian were not remembered for his experimental strategy with armour, he would be celebrated for his demonstration of the potentialities of wireless as a means of command in war.

On the other hand, Guderian was not an easy subordinate. Nor was this the familiar matter of the cleverness of a junior upsetting his less quick or able chief. Several of the officers with whom Guderian fell out were able men: Kluge, for example, was quite the opposite of a fool – the explanation of their bad relations may lie perhaps in a personal incompatibility; Kleist, too, whom he crossed in 1940, was a clever man; and Halder, with whom Guderian eventually had an open breach, was one of the best minds in the German army. One might draw the conclusion that Guderian was an abrasive character. But there is no evidence that he often upset subordinates, in the way that Model was so notorious for doing during those whirlwind tours of his front which he had copied, perhaps, from Guderian. The final answer is probably that he pushed his differences with his seniors to the lengths that he did because he had a sense of being right; that he was, in short, inclined to be doctrinaire – and all the more stubbornly so for having invented the doctrine which he wished to see translated into action.

And what of Guderian as a strategist? Here one enters an area of judgement where firm conclusions are hard to arrive at. The Great Question – that of the strategy of the Russian campaign in July–August 1941 - is endlessly debated; but perhaps the balance of evidence goes to Guderian. For all its risks, and they were immense, an uninterrupted drive on Moscow, at a moment when the Soviet armies, though still strong, were virtually incapable of manoeuvre and when the road lay almost unguarded, might very well have given Hitler the Russian capital that autumn. But whether the Germans could have ridden out the winter in positions so over-extended raises yet further questions to which there can be no definite answer. Guderian's second period at the centre of strategic decision, from July 1944 to March 1945, was not a moment when any German officer could have demonstrated strategic talent. The Bomb Plot had convinced Hitler that the Officer Corps en bloc, and particulatly the General Staff, was as good as traitorous and he would never again delegate any but the most trifling powers to any of its members. He had been directing in person all operations outside Russia before July; thereafter he was to give the same attention to the eastern front, leaving Guderian with no freedom of action and no real duty except that of translating his decisions into orders to the troops. Guderian's one real contribution to the German army's efforts at this stage was to attract to himself the rage which Hitler would otherwise have directed at the harassed and blameless field commanders. It was a consistently courageous role that he played and one which quite gave the lie to those jealous brother-officers who had once been able to console themselves for his rapid promotion over them by the whispered taunt that he was Hitler's man. He never was. Indeed, he was his own man his whole life. It was that, and his single-minded determination to restore the military reputation of the German army which make him one of the most memorable of all its officers.

Guderian in retirement at Schwangau

Bibliography

Panzer Leader General Heinz Guderian (Michael Joseph, 1952)
The Battle for Moscow Albert Seaton (Hart-Davis, 1971)
Panzer Battles Major-General F W von Mellenthin (University of Oklahoma Press, 1955)
The March of Conquest Telford Taylor (Hulton, 1958)
Sword and Swastika Telford Taylor (Gollancz, 1953)
The German Army and the Nazi Party Robert J O'Neill (Cassell, 1966)
The Struggle for Europe Chester Wilmot (Collins, 1952)
Hitler's War Directives H R Trevor-Roper (Sidgwick and Jackson, 1964)